"Using a wide range of historical documents, anecdotal reports of trespasses, abuses, and oppressions, refreshingly humorous analogies, and moving personal stories of resistance and determination, Olsen has created a work of history, intrigue and injustice that informs and engages, is hard to put down—I read it in two days and then read it again—and may help to catalyze a movement in support of Hawaii's equivalent to the movements that freed the former Soviet republics to determine their own paths to the future."

—Ellen LaConte, author of
Life Rules: Why So Much Is Going Wrong Everywhere at Once & How Life Teaches Us to Fix It
and the memoirs *On Light Alone* and *Free Radical.*

"Jon Olsen's *Liberate Hawai'i* is an important contribution to the literature about the occupation of Hawai'i. The evidence is indisputable that the takeover of Hawai'i in 1893 by a small group of American businessmen and the subsequent alleged annexation of Hawai'i by the U.S were fraudulent. Olsen makes his case in clear, readable prose, and then examines the value and practicality of independence, citing the example of Lithuania, which was occupied for 50 years before regaining independence from the Soviet Union."

—Arnold Kotler, Publisher, Koa Press, Kihei, Hawai'i

LIBERATE HAWAI'I!

Renouncing and Defying the Continuing Fraudulent U.S. Claim to the Sovereignty of Hawai'i

JON D. OLSEN

Goose River Press
Waldoboro, Maine

Library of Congress Card Number: 2014901635

ISBN: 978-1-59713-147-6

First Printing, 2014

Cover photo by G. Brad Lewis. Used with permission.

Published by
Goose River Press
3400 Friendship Road
Waldoboro ME 04572
e-mail: gooseriverpress@roadrunner.com
www.gooseriverpress.com

Dedicated to the memory of a few of the pioneers of sovereignty for Hawai'i:

George Helm, Kimo Mitchell, John and Marion Kelly, Soli Niheu, Kawaipuna Prejean, and to the memory of my parents, the late William and Alice Olsen, whose example in conduct taught me the **meaning** of the precious word *"pono"* although they never knew this quintessential Hawaiian word. Nov. 1, 2013

Acknowledgments

I have tried to assemble and present the essential historical and legal research that has been done by activist-scholars in Hawai'i in a manner that explains to American citizens this phenomenal reality of dormant sovereignty, long suppressed or overlooked in history books and classes. The most important source for the 1890s era is that written by Queen Lili'uokalani herself, *Hawaii's Story by Hawaii's Queen.* Likewise the most important contemporary work is the research done by Dr. David Keanu Sai, as presented to the International Court of Arbitration in 2001 at The Hague. It is called *Dominion of the Hawaiian Kingdom.* To both I give my gratitude and aloha.

I appreciate as well the contributions to this work by those who have had the patience to read and to offer both encouragement and constructive criticisms of earlier unpublished versions by, among others, Ian Baldwin, Stef Barley, Clarence (Ku) Ching, James Douglass, Eric Herter, the late Louise Korol, Ellen LaConte, Poka Lainui, Kai Landow, Kay Liss, Prof. Donald Livingston, Sam Low, the late Prof. Thomas Naylor, Claire Mortimer, Leland Philbrick, Belva Ann Prycel, David Keanu Sai, Kirkpatrick Sale, Reine Stewart, Regis Tremblay, and Frances Viglielmo.

I wish to acknowledge as well the important work done by Kuhio Vogeler which parallels my own chapter concerning the similarity of relations between Hawai'i and the U.S. on the one hand, and Lithuania and the late U.S.S.R. on the other. I had already done my research several years before his publication, and have not yet read his work.

I mention it to preclude any possible suggestion that

I had appropriated his work without acknowledgment.

If I have made minor errors in this work, please forgive them as having come from an imperfect author. If I have made significant errors, please call them to my attention. Comments, as long as civil, are welcome. I can be reached at P.O. Box 362, Jefferson, Maine 04348, or by email at joliyoka@gmail.com.

TABLE OF CONTENTS

Forward

In his fascinating new book *Liberate Hawai'i: Renouncing and Defying the Continuing Fraudulent U.S. Claim to the Sovereignty of Hawai'i,* Green Party activist Jon Olsen makes the case that the right question to be asking in these perilous, hyper-partisan times is not whether President Obama was really born in Hawaii (I'll use the conventional, Americanized spelling here, but note that it's a concession to the status quo), but whether Hawaii is really—legally—a state of the union. If one sticks to the letter of the laws that apply to incorporation of new states into the union, Olsen persuades us that it is not. This was news to me and at the outset I was inclined to resist the idea, but the case he makes for it in this eminently readable, thoroughly researched book appears to be inarguable.

While a majority of non-Hawaiian residents of Hawaii voted for statehood, a significant number of Hawaiians stayed home because the vote was either for "statehood" or continued status as a "US Territory," a no-win vote. In the contemporary era, for the last 130 years or so, thousands of Hawaiians have resisted what they consider to be occupation of their islands and misappropriation of their land and resources. The "pro-statehood" vote resulted from continued decline in Native Hawaiian population, 60 years of US-sponsored propaganda, the trauma of the 1941 attack on Pearl Harbor and subsequent war for which the islands were an important staging area, and finally, the lax eligibility rules that allowed for virtually any adult living in Hawaii in 1959 to vote. The result was analogous to the status of Native Americans on the U.S. mainland who were outnumbered and marginalized by the descendants of the continent's colonizers.

Olsen's claim in support of a diverse group of increasingly rebellious islanders, a claim he makes forcefully, is that since proper steps toward statehood were never actually taken, Hawaiians and other sovereignty activists would be well within their rights to demand and lobby for the restoration of their status as a sovereign state. In a well-reasoned final chapter, he lays out the steps those who presently support independence might take to achieve majority support in the islands, in the international community and in the U.S. and to leverage and legitimize their sovereign status.

Given that we associate the occupation and annexation of sovereign states by imperial powers with Nazi Germany and the former Soviet Union—examples Olsen cites to support his contention—the negative implications for U.S. integrity of the American occupation of the Hawaiian islands in the 19th century and coerced statehood in the 20th are many. Chapters detailing egregious military and political conquest of the islands by an expansive, aggressive and deeply unprincipled American Congress eager in the 1890s and by any means to gain a foothold in the Pacific and access to Asian markets, are particularly gripping and embarrassing. Queen Liliuokalani and President Grover Cleveland emerge as unsung heroes in an age of duplicitous and politically corrupt as our own.

Using a wide range of historical documents, anecdotal reports of trespasses, abuses, and oppressions, refreshingly humorous analogies, and moving personal stories of resistance and determination, Olsen has created a work of history, intrigue and injustice that informs and engages, that is hard to put down—I read it in two days and then read it again—and may help to catalyze a movement in support of Hawaii's freedom equivalent to the movements that freed the former Soviet republics to determine their own paths to the future. Residents of continental states who have raised the issue of secession from the U.S. will certainly be drawn to the documents that make the case for restored Hawaiian sovereignty.

Ellen LaConte—author of *Life Rules: Why So Much is Going Wrong Everywhere at Once & How Life Teaches Us to Fix It* and the memoirs *On Light Alone* and *Free Radical.*

Preface

The inquisitive reader can challenge this author, "Who are you, a Caucasian not living in Hawai'i now, not born there, to write such a book and presume to speak for the people of Hawai'i?" My reply is as follows: My work is intended to amplify the voices of people in Hawai'i who are already eloquently speaking up. I am acting in the role of a promoter of the excellent research and commentary already done. However, I will not avoid asserting my own perspective throughout the work. I have attempted to assemble this information in a manner that I trust will be readily understood by people outside Hawai'i. Full credit must go to those steadfast activists and scholarly pioneers in Hawai'i.

Just as some people are highly sensitive to light, shape and color and become artists, while others are unusually sensitive to sound and become musicians, I am unusually sensitive to justice, and I became a political activist. This is what I do, because unless I do act, I am in a state of discontent because I am not doing my part on behalf of justice and truth. Simple as that.

I lived in Hawai'i for 36 years, from 1965 well into 2001, and anticipate a return. I was active with SDS (Students for a Democratic Society), The Resistance (against the Draft), and Peace and Freedom Party, participated in anti-nuclear, anti-imperialist work, and was present during the early days of the protest in Kalama Valley against forced evictions. This confrontation was the first of many land use struggles during the 70s and 80s involving forced evictions of low income people to make way for corporate developers of up-scale housing. I attended for awhile the meetings of the Protect Kaho'olawe Ohana and was a founding member of the Hawai'i Green Party. I formed and ran (along with many other volunteers) a political bookstore from 1971 to 1978 in Honolulu.

Take a look at what some people in Hawai'i have to say about the status of Hawai'i. In 1998 a newsletter called *Self-*

Determination was published to promote sovereignty. The headline quotes boldly and with firm approval the request made of Hawaiians in 1897 by a key leader, James Keauiluna Kaulia, "FOREVER PROTEST THE ANNEXATION OF HAWAI'I."

One of the articles contained in this newsletter addresses the question most readers will have. The title of the article is "The importance of Annexation to Kanaka Maoli today." The phrase Kanaka Maoli means "indigenous Hawaiian people."

Since the article is not long, it will be useful to cite it in its entirety.

> Annexation has had devastating consequences for our Kanaka Maoli people, our identity, our culture, our distinct language, our health, our lands and our spirit as a people. We are still feeling the effects of annexation today.
>
> One of the most important effects of annexation on our people is that it sabotaged our Kanaka Maoli right to self-determination. Without annexation, our Kanaka Maoli people could have continued to rebel against and could have toppled the illegal haole (Note: Caucasian people, originally foreign people--author) government. But annexation meant that the U.S. government had committed itself and its military to forcibly make Hawai'i a territory of the United States. The United States committed itself to continue to back the haole oligarchy who took over our government and our land.
>
> Once Hawai'i became a colonial territory of the United States (note: *de facto* colonial territory, but not *de jure*, or legally established colonial territory—author), restoration of our sovereign nation was made much more difficult. Today, State government officials, the

U.S. military, tourists and settlers from continental United States simply think Hawai'i is theirs, without regard to our Kanaka people and or rights.

The current government of the State of Hawai'i is the modern version of the territorial colonial government that was put into power at annexation. The United States in 1898 appointed Sanford Dole to continue his rule as the first governor and allowed the haole elite and their institutions to become even richer and more powerful. Ever since then, our lives have been controlled by non-Kanaka Maoli people who run the government, control the economy, and exploit our lands and our people.

Annexation was accomplished in large part because of the importance of Pearl Harbor as a base for the U.S. military in its war against Spain (the Spanish-American War). This war allowed the United States to dominate the Philippines and Guam in the Pacific and Puerto Rico and Cuba in the Caribbean. The U.S. military has since increased its presence and has harmed our people, our environment and our Kanaka Maoli people's rights to our land and sovereignty. The U.S. military continues to destroy our Kanaka Maoli sacred cultural and burial sites and use our lands for bombing practice, as it did on Kaho'olawe and today at Makua and Pohakuloa.

Just as a criminal who commits other illegal acts to cover up the first crime, the illegal overthrow and annexation ultimately led to the fraudulent 1959 "plebiscite" vote that made Hawai'i the 50th state of the United States (allegedly—author). The 1959 statehood process did not comply with the rules for decolonization under international law for a free and fair process

> for our Kanaka Maoli people. The result, once again, was that our right to decide the future of our own homeland (our right to self-determination) was violated. (1)

A number of books and articles have been written from the perspective that the central issue is that of oppression of native Hawaiian people, which, of course, is true. Hawaiians have a long list of legitimate grievances against both the federal and "state" governments. Among these grievances since 1893 have been confiscation of land, disrespect of the language and culture, forced assimilation into an alien cultural and economic system, national identify theft, and so on. Often, however, the remedies sought have been relegated to granting (back) of lands and significant monetary compensation, but leaving intact the fundamental social-political order. Recent scholarly research has shown however, that the issue is even larger: armed robbery of a sovereign multiethnic nation, the only just remedy for which is full restoration of national status, with compensation to be negotiated. This will be the line of reasoning of the effort presented here.

The book is intended primarily for American citizens who are likely only vaguely aware of these issues, because this history has never been taught them, secondarily for the broad population of Hawai'i, who have learned some of the basics of these matters, but who have not been exposed to a comprehensive outlook, and thirdly, for Hawaiian activists (who already know most of this information) to use as a tool to reach still others.

During the 19th century, when the central challenge to Hawai'i's sovereignty took place, it was common to capitalize titles like Queen, King, and President, even when preceded by "the." In order to be true to the quotes in this regard, and for editorial simplicity, I have elected to universalize this practice throughout this book. Accordingly, despite being a minor grammatical error, you will find "King," "Queen," and "President" used consistently.

A note on punctuation: In more recent times, with intensification of Hawaiian language studies, more attention has been put on accuracy of the written representation of the language. Two examples stand out in particular. The name of the subject matter of this book is now written Hawai'i, whereas in earlier references it will be written Hawaii. Similarly, the name now written as Lili'uokalani, was formerly written Liliuokalani, which is how it appears in her own book, *Hawaii's Story by Hawaii's Queen.* The difference is the punctuation mark called *'okina*, representing a glottal stop. The example of the sound given in the Pukui and *Elbert New Pocket Hawaiian Dictionary* is to compare it to the English term "oh-oh." In this book, I shall follow the original context in each case. That is, if the words in the manuscript from which I am quoting omit the punctuation, I shall omit it as well. Where it is present, I shall use it. So all through the book, the reader will see Hawaii and also Hawai'i.

Chapter 1

Introduction to the Central Issue

Imagine that around 1900 several thousand Americans migrated to another country, let's say Denmark. They purchased land, learned the language, intermarried with Danish citizens, raised families, and became prosperous significant citizens of the Danish community. Then, decades later, it was the perception of these American-Danish citizens that their growing economic interests would be best served by becoming part of the United States. They began to intrigue to obtain, by virtue of their economic status and shrewd business skills, important positions within the Danish government.

Finally it got to the point, let us say in the year 1993, where these descendants of the original immigrants, together with some who came later, decided to overthrow the Danish government and claim the whole country as U.S. property, and all the citizens now to be no longer Danish, but Americans. As Danish citizens became conscious of this plot to rob them of their sovereignty and natural citizenship, they protested vigorously. They signed petitions by the thousands and were backed up by the Danish government which declared such intrigues to be treasonous.

But the Danish-American businessmen only stepped up their plotting, and appealed to the U.S. government to land troops to protect their lives and property from angry Danes. This was done, and in the process, the Danish government was overthrown and replaced with a "provisional government" consisting of the very perpetrators themselves. They then established a legislative branch, with the important qualification that only those loyal to the new government would be eligible to run for office and vote, thereby disenfranchising the vast majority of Danish citizens. Once done, the perpetrators then appealed to the U.S. for annexation to complete their plot.

After a series of intrigues, Denmark was declared to be American territory in 1998, much to the astonishment and shock of the entire Danish population. The U.S. quickly established military bases to preclude armed resistance by the Danes, and teams of "educators" came to insist that Danes learn English as the language of the country, and that displays of Danish culture would be frowned on and even repressed henceforth.

Preposterous as such a scenario seems, that is just how, 100 years earlier, that is, in 1898, the sovereign nation of Hawai'i was "acquired" by the United States of America. This book will demonstrate just how this came about, and how at every single step of the way, the procedure was fraudulent and illegal, both by accepted international law, and also by U.S. Constitutional law. This is not a mere futile examination of history. I will also address how this betrayal of sovereignty continues today, affecting all residents, but especially Native Hawaiians. I shall ask the readers to keep an open mind as I assert here that the United States, to this very day, has no valid claim to the nation of Hawai'i, with stress on the word "valid."

The original research into archival documents, both Hawaiian and of the United States, has been done by dedicated people in Hawai'i. During the 36 years I lived there, I came to understand and appreciate the magnitude of the betrayal and to unite whole-heartedly with the struggle for sovereignty. I hope fair-minded readers will come to the same conclusions on behalf of justice.

Everyone understands the concept of seniority. If you are in line ahead of others, you have a socially understood right to be served first. If you have held a job for ten years, your pay and benefits are expected to be greater than a newcomer, assuming comparable work responsibilities. Hawaiian citizens were there first, but this seniority has been ignored. In addition to the clear issue of seniority, the legitimacy of a government lies, wisely according to the Declaration of Independence, in "the consent of the governed." The governed in Hawaii never gave their consent to either the overthrow of the Queen or subsequent alleged "annexation." Quite the contrary! As we will see later on, the so-called 1959 plebiscite on statehood was also bogus. Truth, justice, and human rights require that the issue be addressed with honesty.

Most readers, upon sensing the direction of this book, will silently ask the author, "Recognizing that a grave injustice has been done, what does this have to do with contemporary history? After all, isn't this a completed historical matter, rather like the Louisiana Purchase and the acquisition of Alaska?" This of course, is a fair question, one which will be addressed later in some detail. The preliminary answer is to look at the broad sweep of history and realize that on innumerable occasions, what appears to be "a done deal" is far from that! In modern history (avoiding going back to ancient Greece, Rome, and mid-East conquests) there is an abundance of rapid changes in status upon which to draw. The Spanish empire was once enormous, particularly in Central and South America; Indonesia used to be governed by the Dutch; France regarded Algeria as "part of" France; England reigned supreme in India into the 1940's. The South African apartheid regime appeared rock solid. As late as 1985, the U.S.S.R. was regarded by most as immutable. What happened? People make history! They come to the conclusion that the status quo is no longer acceptable. Once one learns of the proud history of Hawai'i as an independent nation, complete with its own currency, embassies and consulates, legal system integrating western ideas with those of centuries of self-rule, and its leading role in developing international law regarding neutrality of states in time of war, one can readily understand the yearning for a proper restoration of independence.

There are two important issues that need to be addressed, although each bears on the other. The first is the question of the *desirability* of regained independent status. The second is the matter of the *feasibility* of such an ambition. When the subject of Hawaiian sovereignty is brought up, even in Hawai'i, frequently the second takes precedence in the minds of the questioners. That sort of thinking short-circuits the first question with words like, "Sure that would be nice, but you know, the United States would never let that happen." Accordingly they dismiss the entire matter as "impractical." In the conventional manner of thinking, they are right, of course. One need not belabor that point. But the point of this book is to think outside the box and not accept "conventional thinking" as the boundary of thought. Rather, the first matter to be addressed is that of a) justification for restoration of sovereignty and b) what benefits could be derived from such a transition. Once these matters are clear, one can then begin to address the second question "How?"

An analogy comes to mind: Suppose a man lives in Massachusetts and his wife proposes, "Let's go to California." Suppose the man just said, "It's too far away; I don't know the way to San Jose; and we can't afford it, anyway." Such thinking short-circuits the rational process of deliberation of the merits of the idea and throws up the obstacles as a smokescreen to further consideration. The result is defeat and discouragement. Of course, in the matter at hand, that is exactly what those promoting the continued occupation of the nation of Hawai'i want—discourage the idea before it can evolve.

The astute reader will no doubt come up with the next challenge: "Do the people of Hawai'i want to be independent of the U.S.?" Once again, this is a valid question, but one with many facets. The preliminary answer is: "Some do, some don't." Those who understand the history are generally advocates; those who do not have this understanding generally would favor the status quo. It is rather like claiming that kidnapping a child was in fact "adopting" the child. Consent was never given! The transition to U.S. control was literally done on the basis of having guns directed at Hawaiian subjects who supported the Queen.

From the macrocosm to the microcosm, let us use an analogy of an extended family. You are part of this family who has lived for generations in an estate with a single mansion and ample grounds for cultivation and with a well for water supply, in short, a self-sustaining community of people. Then one day another family arrives escorted by a dozen policemen who summarily evict you, putting all your precious books, papers, family photographs, furniture, etc. on the lawn outside the house. With the help of the police, the new family takes over your mansion. Obviously, you protest vigorously to the newcomers who are stealing your home from right under your nose, and to the policemen who have helped them. The new "owner" shows you a folder of papers "proving" that he has purchased the home. You stare in disbelief when shown a power-of-attorney document and a deed. The power-of-attorney document gives authority to someone you know but don't trust at all, the right to sell your home, and it has your name forged as an authorization! The supposed "deed" selling your property has been signed by this mistrusted person.

You and your family members protest to the new "owner" that you never agreed to such a document and that it is fraudulent. The "owner" shrugs his shoulders and says, "But I paid for it," and walks inside, closing the door in your face. You then show the documents to the police, but they say, "It's his house now, so you better leave or we will arrest you for trespassing." Your neighbors are as puzzled as you are and are sympathetic, but don't know how to help you. Your next step is to find an attorney, whom you have to pay, and he takes the matter to court. The judge says, "Well, there seems to be some impropriety here, but the transaction is a done deal. I will, however, order the new owner to pay you $300 a month and allow you to put up a small structure at the back of the lot so that your family will have a roof over its heads. Case dismissed." Think about how you would feel then!

Further, one has to factor in the effect of over one hundred years of "colonial" propaganda, not only directed toward generations of people already in Hawai'i, but upon those immigrating to Hawai'i such as Japanese, Chinese, Koreans, Filipinos and Samoans, as well as those who have immigrated to Hawai'i from the U.S. mainland. ("Colonial" is put in quotes to show that, despite the legal reality of occupation, Hawai'i and her people were treated as if it had become a colony.) This legacy of "colonial" mentality is a huge burden to lift, and it takes time. The position of this book is not that a vote today would result in overwhelming support for sovereignty, but that the seeds are there and sprouting, and with proper nourishment, in time will bear abundant fruit.

Chapter 2

Brief Hawaiian History Lesson

Many books have been written about Hawaiian history. This is not the place to replicate what has been done, and certainly not to perpetuate inadequate and misinterpreted versions of Hawaiian history with their common pro-U.S. biases. But it is essential to have some background in Hawaiian history in order to make sense of this presentation. So, students of history, please forgive the highly abbreviated version contained here. I will, however, cover the 1885-1900 years much more closely, for that is the source material for deferred Hawaiian sovereignty. Modern researchers have concluded that the islands of Hawai'i were probably first populated around 200 AD by people migrating from western Pacific Islands, most likely the Marquesas Islands. By then, Polynesian peoples had achieved a remarkable level of navigational ability. Certainly traveling several thousands of miles across open ocean more than a thousand years before Columbus is a remarkable achievement deserving of recognition and admiration in history books.

For some time, scholars had been unwilling to accept that such voyages had been anything but random or accidental. However, the modern interest in open ocean non-instrument navigation got a huge boost in the 1970's when a man named Mau Piailug was discovered living on a remote Micronesian island. This man was one of the last of the master navigators whose skills had been passed down for countless generations. He agreed to be the teacher of a Hawaiian man named Nainoa Thompson, who himself under the guidance of Mau Piailug, became a master navigator in the ancient tradition. In 1976, together with his teacher, he successfully navigated, without instruments, the return trip of the double-hulled canoe *Hokule'a* from Tahiti to Hawai'i, after Mau Piailug had navigated the Hawai'i to Tahiti journey, one of many such voyages to be made to and from the South Pacific. (1) The most difficult of these culminated in 1999 with a voyage east to tiny Rapanui, otherwise known as Easter Island, off the coast of South America.

As a result of numerous voyages by the early Polynesian settlers from the Marquesas and from Tahiti, to the formerly unpopulated (by humans) Hawaiian Islands, a thriving population grew on the fertile land with abundant sea life all around. Not only were ancient Hawaiians superb navigators, but they evolved sophisticated engineering feats of water management, directing the natural flow of water from mountain streams into large numbers of irrigation channels. The people were large, powerful, and healthy, and had an excellent diet. They evolved a strict but unifying culture which in the main served them well. They had no written language, but developed an extensive oral history tradition. After the arrival of missionaries in the early 1800s, the latter were often astonished at the feats of memory performed by Hawaiians, such as reciting entire chapters of the Bible shortly after having been introduced to it. Most important for Hawaiians was their story of Creation and their own evolution and genealogy contained in their sacred chant (their method of recounting their stories) *The Kumulipo*. This vital story was later written and translated by Queen Lili'uokalani, the last of the Hawaiian monarchs prior to the alleged "annexation" in order that it not be lost as Hawaiian numbers diminished and ancient ways and knowledge forgotten.

The first people of European descent to arrive in Hawai'i, quite by accident, were the crew of the ships directed by Englishman Capt. James Cook, with his first encounter in 1778, only two years after the Declaration of Independence by the U.S. colonies. The Revolutionary War was occurring simultaneously with this discovery. Cook named his discovery "The Sandwich Islands" after his patron, the Earl of

Sandwich. Cook returned two more times, and on the third was killed in battle. It was during these visitations that venereal and other diseases, such as leprosy (now known as Hansen's disease) came to the Hawaiian people, who had little immunity to them. Consequently, large numbers succumbed, and the population dropped precipitously.

Not long after initial contacts were made, an active trade began, with Hawai'i as a base between North America and Asia. Whalers made regular hunts into Hawaiian waters, as whales migrated to warmer waters to give birth each year. Fragrant sandalwood forests were decimated for the economic benefit of foreigners. Modeled after European royalty, Hawai'i evolved a monarchy, beginning in 1810 with the conquest of or surrender to the powerful warrior Kamehameha the First. Under British influence, Kamehameha adopted some of the formality and ceremonial features of British royalty. Absolute rule was voluntarily relinquished by King Kamehameha III on October 8, 1840, initiating a constitutional monarchy, with executive, legislative, and judiciary powers. (2)

Shortly after the evolution to a constitutional monarchy, a threat to the sovereignty of the Kingdom developed. Lord George Paulet of Great Britain attempted to claim The Sandwich Islands for England, and threatened force to implement such jurisdiction. Judiciously, King Kamehameha III agreed to abstain from battle, allowing the British delegation to assume temporary authority, pending appeal to the English government. Admiral Sir Richard Thomas rebuked the officer and restored authority to the King. (3) This example was to play a pivotal role 50 years later when a nearly identical situation arose, but with the United States rather than England. The consequence were far different. In 1842,

> To counter the strong possibility of foreign encroachment on Hawaiian territory, His Majesty King Kamehameha III dispatched a Hawaiian delegation to

the United States and Europe to settle differences with other nations and negotiate treaties. This delegation's ultimate duty was to secure the recognition of Hawaiian Independence from the major powers of the world. (4)

This mission was accomplished by securing "the assurance of United States' President Tyler that the United States would recognize Hawaiian independence. The delegation then proceeded to meet their colleague, Sir George Simpson, in Europe and together they secured formal recognition from Great Britain and France." (5)

"On November 28, 1843, at the Court of London, the British and French Governments entered into a joint agreement for the recognition of Hawaiian independence. The Proclamation reads as follows:

> Her Majesty the Queen of the United Kingdom of Great Britain and Ireland, and His Majesty the King of the French, taking into consideration the existence in the Sandwich Islands of a government capable of providing for the regularity of its relations with foreign nations, have thought it right to engage, reciprocally, to consider the Sandwich Islands as an Independent State, and never to take possession, neither directly or under the title of Protectorate, or under any other form, or any part of the territory of which they are composed. (6)

Similar treaties directly or implicitly, via trade agreements, recognizing independence and sovereignty of the Sandwich Islands as the Kingdom of Hawaii were recorded as follows: (all citations: *Dominion of the Hawaiian Kingdom)*

Austria-Hungary June 18, 1875 (II.1. a. 2.1)
Belgium October 4, 1862 (II 1.b 2.2, 2.3)
Denmark October 19, 1846 (II.1.d 2.7, 2.8)
Germany March 25, 1879 (II 1,.f 2.15, 2.16)
Italy July 22, 1863 (II.1.i 2.26, 2.27)
Japan August 19, 1871 (II.1.j 2.29, 2.30)
Netherlands October 16, 1862 (II.1.k 2.32, 2.33)
Russia June 19, 1869 (II.1.m 2.38, 2.39)
Spain October 29, 1863 (II 1.o 2.43, 2.44)
Swiss Confederation July 20, 1864 (II.1. p 2.46, 2.47)
Sweden and Norway July 1, 1852 (II.1.q 2.48, 2.49)

In each of these cases, along with many others which could be cited, *none of the parties* have given notice of their intentions to terminate these treaties (identical references as above cited). Accordingly, a legal case can be made that these treaties *remain in effect*, though in suspended animation, as a result of the consequences of the events of the 1890s and since.

To the point, "On December 20, 1849, the Treaty between the United States of America and the Hawaiian Kingdom was concluded and signed in Washington, D.C.. Ratifications by both countries were exchanged in Honolulu on the Island of O'ahu, on August 24, 1850. Article VIII of the treaty provides:

> '. . .each of the two contracting parties engages that the citizens or subjects of the other residing in their respective States shall enjoy their property and personal security as in full and ample manner as their own citizens or subjects, or the subjects or citizens of the most favored nations, but subject always to the laws and statutes of the two countries respectively.'

"In addition, Article XVI of the said treaty provides that any:

'. . .citizen or subject of either party infringing the articles of this treaty shall be held responsible for the same, and the harmony and good correspondence between the two governments shall not be interrupted thereby, each party engaging in no way to protect the offender, or sanction such violation.' (7)

"Neither the United States nor the Hawaiian Kingdom gave notice to the other of its intention to terminate this treaty in accordance with terms of Article XVI of the 1849 Treaty. Therefore the treaty is still in full force, continues to have legal effect until today . . ." (8)

During the years subsequent to 1845, there came into existence a system of land tenure which heretofore had been alien to Hawaiians, fee ownership and the right to inheritance. Prior to this, use of the land had been communal under the authority of the King and chiefs of respective land areas known as *ahupua'a*—districts reaching from mountains through the respective valleys down to the ocean shore. Aspects of the relationship between commoners and *ali'i* (the class of chiefs prior to the European introduced concept of royalty, which then was included under the *ali'i* category) bore a resemblance to feudal societies.

Hawaiian land was divided into three categories: that which continued to be vested in the monarch, called Crown lands, that which was claimed (with evidence) by chiefs, and that claimed by virtue of regular and customary use by ordinary Hawaiians. This division, initiated in 1848, with several years to administer, has been known since as the Great *Mahele.*

The Hawaiian government of the 1850s was a major player in the development of modern protocols of neutrality in time of war. Significant official correspondence took place among England, France, Russia, the United States, and the Hawaiian Kingdom. Of particular relevance is an exchange between the United States and the Hawaiian Kingdom:

"On December 5, 1854, the U.S. Commissioner assigned

to the Hawaiian Kingdom, His Excellency David L Gregg, sent the following dispatch to the Hawaiian Kingdom government regarding the recognition of neutral rights. The correspondence stated, in part,

> '. . .I have the honor to transmit to you a project of a declaration in relation to neutral rights which my government has instructed me to submit to the consideration of the government of Hawai'i, and respectfully to request its approval and adoption. . .' (9)

"After careful review of the U.S. President's request, the Hawaiian Kingdom Government, by His Majesty King Kamehameha IV in Privy Council, passed the following resolution on March 26, 1855.

> 'Resolved: That the Declaration of accession to the principles of neutrality to which the President of the United States invites the King, is approved, and Mr. Wyllie is authorized to sign and seal the same and pass it officially to the Commissioner of the United States in reply to his dispatches of the 6th of December and 12th of January last.' (10)

"On April 7, 1855, His Majesty King Kamehameha IV opened the Legislative Assembly. In that speech he reiterated the Kingdom's neutrality by stating, in part,

> 'It is gratifying to me, on commencing my reign, to be able to inform you that my relations with all the great Powers, between whom and myself exist treaties of amity, are of the most satisfactory nature. I have received from all of them, assurances that leave no room to doubt that my rights and sovereignty will be respected. My policy, as regards all foreign nations, being that of peace, impartiality and neutrality, in the

> spirit of the Proclamation by the late king of 16th May last, and of the Resolutions of the Privy Council of the 15th June and 17th July. . . .' (11)

In 1864, a new Constitution was put into practice by the new King, Kamehameha V. An important provision "preventing any future Monarch of the right to alter the constitution without the approval of two-thirds of all members of the Legislative Assembly." (12) This provision is significant with regards to the events of the 1880s and 1890s.

Meanwhile, the descendants of early missionaries, traders, and businesspeople, along with some who had migrated to Hawaii later from the U.S. and other countries, had begun to chafe under the preponderance of Native Hawaiians in government, and were eager to have more direct political power. Sugar planters, among others, wanted closer ties to the U.S.. Military officers of the United States saw the potential of Pearl Harbor as a major base of operations. By 1874, the Hawaiian throne was vacant, since King Lunalilo had not named a successor prior to his abrupt death. An election in the Legislative Assembly was held and was won by David Kalakaua, who held the throne until his own death in 1891, whereupon his designated successor, his sister, Lydia Kamaka'eha Lili'uokalani, became Queen. (13)

A small number of insurgents organized during the 1880s to gain more direct power, under the name the "Honolulu Rifles." In so doing, this secret all-white organization usurped the name of a previous regular Hawaiian militia. In July of 1887, these individuals forced Kalakaua to accept a new Cabinet Council, and shortly thereafter, forced a new constitution upon the King. The nature of the force used to secure his assent is made clear by Lili'uokalani:

> And now, without any provocation on the part of the King, having matured their plans in secret, the men of foreign birth rose one day *en masse*, called a public

> meeting, and forced the King, without any appeal to the suffrages of the people, to sign a constitution of their own preparation, a document which deprived the sovereign of all power, made him a mere tool in their hands, and practically took away the franchise from the Hawaiian race. This constitution was never in any way ratified, either by the people, or by their representatives, even after violence had procured the King's signature to it. . . .
>
> It may be asked, 'Why did the King give them his signature?" I answer without hesitation, because he had discovered traitors among his most trusted friends, and knew not in whom he could trust; and because he had every assurance, short of actual demonstration, that the conspirators were ripe for revolution, and had taken measures to have him assassinated if he refused. . . .It has been known ever since that day as 'The Bayonet Constitution,' and the name is well chosen. . . . (14)

"Under this so-called constitution a new Legislature was elected while the lawful Legislature remained out of session. The voters, which for the first time included aliens, *had to swear an oath to support the so-called constitution before they could vote."* (Author's emphasis) "The insurgents used the alien vote to offset the majority vote of the aboriginal Hawaiian population, in order to gain control of the Legislative Assembly." (15) The imposed constitution violated both content and procedural aspects of the 1864 constitution. Without doubt, such maneuvering constituted gross interference with the rights of a sovereign country to govern itself.

A broad range of commercial, postal, and related treaties were also in effect during the second half of the nineteenth century. Hawai'i had its own currency and its own Hawaiian language. No one could possibly have mistaken Hawai'i for anything but a sovereign nation prior to 1890. Thus, with all these features in place, Hawai'i had a definitive case for sovereignty *in every respect* going into the 1890s. Yet, as was the case with regard to Native American tribes and nations, when agreements demanding mutual respect, peace, and neutrality stood in the way of imperialist expansion, treaties honoring these values entered into in good faith provided no barrier to expansion.

Chapter 3

The 1893 Sneak Attack Overthrow

Following the death of King David Kalakaua in San Francisco in January of 1891, the heir apparent Queen Lili'uokalani was sworn in under the despised "Bayonet Constitution." As she herself put it, ". . .I was compelled to take the oath to the constitution, the adoption of which had led to my brother's death." (1) She does not elaborate on this charge, but given her earlier testimony about threats against his life, the implication is that he had been murdered while away. Faced with intrigue on many sides and having to endure the sudden loss of her beloved brother, as well as her husband, John Owen Dominis, of natural causes seven months later, the Queen nonetheless, attempted to rise to the occasion and fulfill her duties to the people of Hawai'i, who held her in great respect. Pressed on one side by *coup* plotters, including some among the government itself, and on the other side by the urgent demand of numerous Hawaiian citizens for restoration of the valid 1864 constitution and a voiding of the imposed constitution of 1887, Queen Lili'uokalani had decided to act in favor of her people's wishes.

> On January 14, 1893, Her Hawaiian Majesty Queen Lili'uokalani summoned into the throne room of the Palace, the diplomatic corp, members of the Supreme Court and the Legislative Assembly, as well as a committee of the Hawaiian Political Association, which comprised of aboriginal Hawaiian subjects vehemently opposed to the so-called constitution as evidenced by a multitude of signature petitions the organization had collected. Her Majesty's intention on this day was to

reaffirm the 1864 Constitution as counter to the so-called 1887 Constitution.

This action, on the part of the Queen, generated excitement amongst a minority of the non-aboriginal Hawaiian subjects and alien community, who were co-conspirators in the so-called 1887 constitution that illegally allowed aliens to vote in Kingdom elections. This faction would convince the Queen's ministers to delay her announcement in order to formulate a counter. Thereafter, the Queen regrettably informed her guests that she yielded under the advice of her ministers and promised that on some future day a new constitution would be sought.

In response to the Queen's delay, a meeting of approximately fifty to one hundred people, primarily resident aliens, met at a private office in Honolulu and selected a so-called Committee of Safety, which comprised of thirteen individuals. The national breakdown of this so-called committee was: (6) Hawaiian subjects, not of the aboriginal race, (5) American citizens, (1) British subject, and (1) German citizen. Between the 14th and 16th of January, 1893 the committee had been meeting with the United States Minister assigned to the Hawaiian Kingdom, His Excellency John Stevens, to formulate a plan of annexing the Hawaiian Islands to the United States.

On January 16, 1893 a meeting was organized by the so-called Committee of Safety to protest the Queen's efforts to nullify the illegal constitution of 1887. Continuing to mask their true intentions, the committee sought to procure a resolution to be passed by those in attendance that would denounce the Queen and empower the committee.

On that same day the so-called committee, which was comprised of only five (5) Americans out of thirteen (13), sent a note to the United States Minister purporting that American lives and property were in danger and concluded that,

'We are unable to protect ourselves without the aid, and therefore pray for the protection of United States forces.' (2)

Thereafter, between the hours of 4 and 5 p.m., an invasion force of over 160 well-armed U.S. troops, with two (2) pieces of artillery, were landed and marched through the streets of Honolulu to a position previously selected by Minister Stevens on January 16, 1893."(Author's note: that is, the landing took place on this date, not the selection of the location by Minister Stevens.) The location of the detachment was directly across the Government building and in plain view of the Palace.

Immediately following the unprovoked landing of the American troops, the governor of the island of O'ahu, His Excellency Archibald Cleghorn, sent a communication to the U.S. Minister protesting the landing of troops and called it an unwarranted invasion of Hawaiian soil. At the same time the Hawaiian Minister of Foreign Affairs, His Excellency Samuel Parker, sent a communication to the U.S. Minister and demanded an explanation for the landing of American troops. The U.S. Minister evaded both communications. . . . (3)

That the true intent was to provide armed assistance to the *coup* plotters, and not for the protection of American citizens and businesses, none of which had been threatened by Hawaiian subjects, is made clear by the military assessment provided to U.S. Special Investigator James Blount months later by Rear Admiral Skerrett, ranking officer of the U.S. Naval Force in the Pacific.

> In my opinion it was unadvisable to locate the troops there, if they were landed for the protection of the United States citizens, being distantly removed from the business portion of the town, and generally far away from the United States legation and consulate-general, as well as being distant from the houses and residences of Unites States citizens. . . (4)

Although precise details of the deployment of forces are available in historical documents with references to specific buildings and location of specific people at certain times, for the purposes of this narrative, the focus is on the principal events and some of the commentary of the Queen to the events shortly after they transpired.

When confronted by a determined effort by the conspirators and the armed power of the United States, and upon being assured that she could file an appeal with the authorities in Washington, D.C., and in order to avoid bloodshed, the Queen made the following statement:

> I, Liliuokalani, by the Grace of God and under the constitution of the Hawaiian Kingdom, Queen, do hereby solemnly protest against any and all acts done against myself and the constitutional Government of the Hawaiian Kingdom by certain persons claiming to have established a Provisional Government of and for this Kingdom. That I yield to the superior force of the United States of America, whose Minister Plenipotentiary, His Excellency John L. Stevens, has caused United States troops to be landed at Honolulu, and declared that he would support the said

Provisional Government. Now, to avoid any collision of armed forces, and perhaps loss of life, I do, this under this protest and impelled by said forces, yield my authority until such time as the Government of the United States shall, upon the facts being presented to it, undo the action of its representative, and reinstate me in the authority which I claim as the constitutional sovereign of the Hawaiian Islands.

Done at Honolulu this seventeenth day of January, AD 1893. (5)

This statement is probably the most important made in her lifetime, so it is necessary to read it closely. She gave no credibility whatsoever to the tiny group of conspirators claiming to be the "government of Hawai'i." She surrendered *conditionally and temporarily to the United States* until the facts were reviewed and actions taken to reinstate her, and by *implication,* her successors, to the position to which she had rightly held and which was recognized by the overwhelming majority of Hawai'i's people of all nationalities. Queen Lili'uokalani was following the (then) successful example of King Kamehameha III fifty years before, when he had also conditionally and temporarily surrendered to the British officer Lord Paulet, referenced earlier, whose action was subsequently repudiated by the British government. That government, acting honorably, acknowledged the King's legitimate claim and apologized for the intrusive and unjustified actions of Lord Paulet. This pending claim by Queen Lili'uokalani *remains valid up to and including the present time,* for there is no statute of limitations on the burglary of sovereignty. More on this issue later.

On January 19, 1893, individuals representing the self-proclaimed provisional government sailed for the United States on a steamer especially chartered for the occasion. They arrived in San Francisco on January 28th, and later arrived in Washington, D.C. on February 3rd. On February 14th, 1893, a treaty of annexation was signed between the self-proclaimed provisional government and the United States' Secretary of State under the Harrison administration. The United States assumed it was a popular revolt in the islands and that no troops or officers of the United States were present or took part in the uprising. On February 15th, 1893, this treaty of annexation was submitted to the United States Senate for ratification. Thereafter, the United States Presidency changed with President Grover Cleveland succeeding President Benjamin Harrison. (6)

As it turned out, this change in presidency was highly beneficial to the Hawaiian cause, for the new president was eager to have an honest assessment made of the situation, since communications did not allow for factual checking with varying sources upon receipt of such news.

Upon receipt of Her Majesty's protest, newly elected President Grover Cleveland, on March 9, 1893, withdrew the treaty of annexation from the United States Senate. President Cleveland then dispatched a personal representative to Hawai'i to investigate impartially the causes of the so-called revolution. The representative was to report back to President Cleveland with his findings. President Cleveland would then review the report before deciding whether or not to re-submit the treaty of annexation. Former United States Congressman James Blount conducted the official report of this Presidential established investigation. (7)

It will be useful here to include Queen Lili'uokalani's own assessment of Mr. Blount's investigation, as it is in marked contrast to her assessment of a number of other officials:

> Of the manner in which Hon. J. H. Blount conducted the investigation, I must speak in the terms of the highest praise. He first met the parties opposed to my government, and took down their statements, which were freely given, because they had imagined that he could be easily turned in their favor. So they gave him the truth, and some important facts in admission of their revolutionary intentions, dating from several years back. Mr. Blount afterwards took the statements of the government, or royalist side. These were simply given, straightforward, and easily understood. Compare the two statements, and it is not difficult to explain the final report of Mr. Blount. (8)

A substantial multi-page excerpt from the Queen's statement to James Blount is cited in Appendix B of *Hawaii's Story by Hawaii's Queen.* For our purposes a shorter excerpt will suffice. She speaks of an occasion when she had occasion to speak privately with her brother, King Kalakaua, on the morning of Nov. 26, 1890, shortly before his fateful trip to San Francisco, from which he would not return alive. On this occasion he provided her with information about the precarious condition of his authority. In her words:

> He told me of things that had transpired a few months back. That some of the ministers had thrown guns and ammunition into the sea from the steamer Waimanalo. It was done to prevent him from having them, and had evidently been directed by the reform party, with whom a portion of his ministers were in accord, instead of keeping them for his protection and safety. These ministers were working with a party of conspirators, who are the very same parties who have been the means of the overthrow of my government on the 17th of

> January, 1893. They are called the missionary or reform party. The King went on to say that his guards had been reduced to twenty men, and they were barely sufficient to protect me if there should be any disturbance. . . . It was an insult by his cabinet; and he felt keenly his weakness, that he had no more power or influence since his cabinet was working against him. He explained all these things because he wanted me to study my situation so as to be able to cope with it. (9)

After several paragraphs of explanation of precisely which parties she felt she could trust and who were apparently part of the conspiracy, citing specific incidents, occasions, and even specific conversations, the Queen brought Mr. Blount up to the fateful date of January 17, 1893. She mentioned that she had been fully prepared on January 14th to promulgate a new constitution, which had been widely requested by the people. However, several members of her cabinet advised strongly against it at that time, so she deferred action temporarily, allowing their trap to spring shut three days later. During the next two days, the conspirators finalized their plans to depose the Queen, enlisting the direct support of U.S. military personnel in order to preclude armed resistance.

Ministers of the Queen, even on Monday, the 16th of January,

> gave assurances that any changes desired in fundamental law of the land would be sought only by methods provided in the constitution itself, and signed by myself and ministers. It was intended to reassure the people that they might continue to maintain order and peace.

At about five P.M., however, the troops from the United States ship Boston were landed, by the order of the United States minister, J. L.. Stevens, in secret understanding with the revolutionary party, whose names are (The Queen lists fourteen names, including L. A. Thurston, cited later in this book and S. B. Dole, who went on to become the head of the "Provisional Government," which converted itself into the "Republic of Hawai'i—author's note). Why had they landed when everything was at peace? I was told that it was for the safety of American citizens and the protection of their interests. Then, why had they not gone to the residences, instead of drawing in line in front of the palace gates, with guns pointed at us, and when I was living with my people in the palace? Tuesday morning, at nine o'clock, Mr. S. M. Damon called at the palace. He told me that he had been asked to join a revolutionary council, but that he had declined. He asked me what he should do, and whether he should join the advisory or executive council, suggesting that perhaps he could be of service to me; so I told him to join the advisory council. I had no idea that they intended to establish a new government.

At about two-thirty P.M. Tuesday, the establishment of the Provisional Government was proclaimed; and nearly fifteen minutes later Mr. J. S. Walker came and told me 'that he had come on a painful duty, that the opposition party had requested that I should abdicate.' I told him I had no idea of doing so. . . . The situation being taken into consideration, it was found that, since the troops of the United States had been landed to support the revolutionists, by the order of the American minister, it would be impossible for us to make any resistance. (10)

Subsequent to the temporary overthrow and to the report of James Blount, personal representative of President Cleveland, negotiations between the two heads of state reveal a mutual desire to reestablish the legitimate constitutional monarchy that reigned prior to Jan. 17, 1893. Upon receipt of the fair-minded Blount report, Secretary of State W. H.. Gresham wrote to President Cleveland:

> A careful consideration of the facts will, I think, convince you that the treaty which was withdrawn from the Senate for further consideration should not be resubmitted for its action thereon. Should not the great wrong done to a feeble but independent State by an abuse of the authority of the United States be undone by restoring the legitimate government? Anything short of that will not, I respectfully submit, satisfy the demands of justice. Can the United States consistently insist that other nations shall respect the independence of Hawai'i while not respecting it themselves? Our government was the first to recognize the independence of the Islands and it should be the last to acquire sovereignty over them by force and fraud. (11)

Continuing in the same train of thought, Mr. Gresham directed new United States Minister to Hawai'i Albert Willis (replacing the conspirator John Stevens):

> On your arrival at Honolulu you will take advantage of an early opportunity to inform the Queen of this determination, making known to her the President's sincere regret that the reprehensible conduct of the American minister and the unauthorized presence on land of a military force of the United States obliged her to surrender her sovereignty, for the time being, and rely on the justice of this government to undo the flagrant

> wrong. You will, however, at the same time inform the Queen that, when reinstated, the President expects that she will pursue a magnanimous course of granting full amnesty to all who participated in the movement against her, including persons who are, or who have been, officially or otherwise, connected with the Provisional Government, depriving them of no right or privilege which they enjoyed before the so-called revolution. All obligations created by the Provisional Government in due course of administration should be assumed. (12)

The Queen was faced with an ultimatum, albeit one which, if accepted, would have committed the United States to her restoration. Yet how could she, with limited authority, not being an absolute monarch, unilaterally agree to total amnesty for those who had sought her overthrow on behalf of a foreign power, generally defined as treason? She sought clarification by the President through Minister Willis, and received the following response on December 3, 1893:

> Should the Queen refuse assent to the written conditions, you will at once inform her that the President will cease interposition in her behalf, and that while he deems it his duty to endeavor to restore to the sovereign the constitutional government of the islands, his further efforts in that direction will depend upon the Queen's unqualified agreement that all obligations created by the Provisional Government in a proper course of administration shall be assumed and upon such pledges by her as will prevent the adoption of any measures or proscription or punishment for what has been done in the past by those setting up or supporting the Provisional Government. The President feels that by our original interference and what followed we have incurred responsibilities to the whole Hawaiian

> community, and it would not be just to put one party at the mercy of the other. Should the Queen ask whether if she accedes to conditions active steps will be taken by the United States to effect her restoration or to maintain her authority thereafter, you will say that the President can not use force without the authority of Congress. Should the Queen accept conditions and the Provisional Government refuse to surrender, you will be governed by previous instructions. If the Provisional Government asks whether the United States will hold the Queen to fulfillment of stipulated conditions, you will say, the President, acting under the dictates of honor and duty as he has done to effect restoration, will do all in his constitutional power to cause observance of the conditions he has imposed. (13)

Placed between the proverbial rock and a hard place, the Queen agreed to a conditional amnesty for the conspirators, which fell short of the total amnesty required by President Cleveland. With the fate of her nation hanging in the balance, she wrote to Minister Willis the following short letter on Dec. 18, 1893, in which one can see the indications of her dilemma and intense desire to do what was right.

> Since I had the interview with you this morning I have given the most careful and conscientious thought as to my duty, and I now of my own free will give my conclusions. I must not feel vengeful to any of my people. If I am restored by the United States I must forget myself and remember only my dear people and my country. I must forgive and forget the past, permitting no proscription or punishment of any one, but trusting that all will hereafter work together in peace and friendship for the good and for the glory of our beautiful and once happy land. Asking you to bear to the President and to the Government he represents a message of gratitude

from me and from my people, and promising, with God's grace, to prove worthy of the confidence and friendship of your people. (14)

The Queen's formal acceptance of President Cleveland's conditions, made the same day, read as follows:

> I, Lili'uokalani, in recognition of the high sense of justice which has actuated the President of the United States, and desiring to put aside all feelings of personal hatred or revenge and to do what is best for all the people of these Islands, both native and foreign born, do hereby and herein solemnly and pledge myself that, if reinstated as the constitutional sovereign of the Hawaiian Islands, that I will immediately proclaim and declare, unconditionally and without reservation, to every person who directly or indirectly participated in the revolution of January 17, 1893, a full pardon and amnesty for their offenses, with restoration of all rights, privileges, and immunities under the constitution and the laws which have been made in pursuance thereof, and that I will forbid and prevent the adoption of any measures of proscription or punishment for what has been done in the past by those setting up or supporting the Provisional Government. (15)

By coincidence, the same day that Queen Lili'uokalani was formulating her official acceptance of rather onerous conditions as the better of two rather unpalatable options, President Cleveland, some six thousand miles away, gave a major address to Congress on the matter of Hawai'i, using the Blount report as his foundation. In that December 18th, 1893 speech to Congress he made the following points, among others (see Appendix A for the complete speech):

Our country was in danger of occupying the position of having actually set up a temporary government on foreign soil for the purpose of acquiring through that agency territory which we had wrongfully put in its possession. The control of both sides of a bargain acquired in such a manner is called by a familiar and unpleasant name when found in private transactions. . . .

I believe that a candid and thorough examination of the facts will force the conviction that the provisional government owes its existence to an armed invasion by the United States. Fair-minded people with the evidence before them will hardly claim that the Hawaiian Government was overthrown by the people of the islands or that the provisional government had ever existed with their consent. . . . But for the notorious predilections of the United States Minister for annexation, the Committee of Safety, which should be called the Committee of Annexation, would never have existed. . . . . But for the landing of the United States forces upon false pretexts respecting the danger to life and property the committee would never have exposed themselves to the pains and penalties of treason by undertaking the subversion of the Queen's Government. . . . And finally, but for the lawless occupation of Honolulu under false pretexts by the United States forces, and but for Minister Stevens' recognition of the provisional government when the United States forces were its sole support and constituted its only military strength, the Queen and her Government would never have yielded to the provisional government, even for a time and for the sole purpose of submitting her case to the enlightened justice of the United States. . . . By an act of war, committed with the participation of a diplomatic representative of the

> United States and without authority of Congress, the Government of a feeble but friendly and confiding people has been overthrown. A substantial wrong has thus been done which a due regard for our national character as well as the rights of the injured people requires that we should endeavor to repair. . . . When our Minister recognized the provisional government the only basis upon which it rested was the fact that the Committee of Safety had in the manner above stated declared it to exist. It was neither a government de facto nor de jure. That it was not in such possession of the Government property and agencies as entitled it to recognition is conclusively proved by a note found in the files of the legation at Honolulu, addressed by the declared head of the provisional government to Minister Stevens. . . . (16)

President Cleveland continued by pointing out that the surrender of the Queen had been not to the provisional government, but temporarily and conditionally to the United States until the matter could be fairly reviewed. Furthermore, since it was the declared intention of the provisional government to seek annexation, and that even further, that the very reason for the existence of this provisional government was annexation, then denial of annexation by the U.S., which President Cleveland insisted would be the case, denied also the purpose of the illegitimate provisional government, and accordingly citizens anticipated the restoration of the monarchy. (17) As the Provisional Government categorically refused to relinquish its claims to power, the result was a standoff for the remainder of the Cleveland presidency.

The illegality of the claim by the conspirators to be the government of Hawai'i should be obvious to any fair-minded person. Except for the intervention of the U.S. minister and by his order the landing of heavily armed troops, the insurgents would easily have been routed by the indignant population. James Blount, President Cleveland's personal investigator, and the American who probably understood the situation better than anyone external to Hawai'i, had this to say in a letter to the U.S. Secretary of State:

> . . .the fact that the landing of the troops under existing circumstances could, according to all law and precedent, be done only on the request of the existing Government, having failed in utilizing the Queen's cabinet, resorted to the new device of a committee of safety, made of Germans, British, Americans, and natives of foreign origin, led and directed by two native subjects of the Hawaiian Islands. With these leaders, subjects of the Hawaiian Islands, the American minister consulted freely as to the revolutionary movement and gave them assurance of protection from danger at the hands of the royal Government and forces. (18)

So what we have is a shell game wherein the conspirators pretend to be a new government and ask for recognition *from the very power* that had conspired with them, and without which power they would have been immediately defeated. This is a perfect example of a puppet regime. "A puppet regime is the organ of the occupant and any agreement or agreements made between them is really an agreement made by the occupants with themselves, as the puppet government can possess no standing under international law as a contracting party." (19) Subsequent declarations that converted this illegitimate puppet government (Provisional Government) into the "Republic of Hawaii" with essentially the same cast of characters by no means provides any authority to "cede" an entire nation (Hawai'i) to another (United States), forfeiting the sovereignty of all the citizens to self-determination. The analogy cited at the beginning of this book is apt: it is like a forged power-of-attorney document, which is then used to sign away ownership of a house (or in this case, nation). This ploy was transparent to the Cleveland administration, which continued to refuse to grant any credibility to the usurpers.

Nonetheless, this band of insurgents was unwilling to grant the Queen the same respect and humanity she had been willing, under duress, to give them. After declaring martial law, they arrested her on January 16, 1895 (two years minus one day after they had betrayed her) and charged her with treason, and the next day set up a court martial trial. A week later, on January 24, 1895, while in prison and faced with the threat of execution of her supporters, she was forced to sign a document "abdicating the throne." (20) Rationalized beyond credibility to avoid having to use words like conquer, plunder, and betrayal, U.S. government policy has violated the spirit and the letter of international treaties, as the remainder of this work will show.

Chapter 4

Her Majesty, the Queen

A work on the critical period of 1890 to 1900 would be incomplete without some attempt to convey the extraordinary character of the central figure of the time, Queen Lili'uokalani. This writer has been deeply impressed with the depth of her wisdom, compassion, and grace, and her superb command of the English language as she described both her deep gratitude for the loyalty not only of her people but of those non-native Hawaiians and the anti-imperialist Americans who understood the anguish of the betrayal she suffered. Her choice of words to describe those who committed that betrayal is both eloquent and tactful. Here will be included but a few relevant quotations from her important book, *Hawaii's Story by Hawaii's Queen*, originally published in the vitally important year of 1898. These selections can only increase the reader's empathy with this woman who endured the dismantling of her civilization while being stifled in her pursuit of truth and justice at every turn, not the least by the American media, during her attempts to explain the Hawaiian situation.

"I have had no experiences more painful than the evidences of ingratitude among those I have had reason to think my friends. . . ." (1)

She sums up the reign of her brother, King David Kalakaua, who suffered indignities on the part of the "missionary party."

> It is more to the point that Kalakaua's reign was, in a material sense, the golden age of Hawaiian history. The wealth and importance of the Islands enormously increased, and always as a direct consequence of the

> King's acts. It has currently been supposed that the policy and foresight of the 'missionary party' is to be credited with all that he accomplished, since they succeeded in abrogating so many of his prerogatives, and absorbing the lion's share of the benefits derived from it. It should, however, be only necessary to remember that the measures which brought about our accession of wealth were not at all in line with a policy of annexation to the United States, which was the very essence of the dominant 'missionary' idea. In fact, his progressive foreign policy was well calculated to discourage it.
>
> And for this reason, probably, they could not be satisfied even with the splendid results which our continued nationality offered them. They were not grateful for a prosperity which must sooner or later, while enriching them, also elevate the masses of the Hawaiian people into a self-governing class, and depose them from that primacy in our political affairs which they chiefly valued. They became fiercely jealous of every measure which promised to benefit the native people, or to stimulate their national pride. Every possible embarrassment and humiliation were heaped upon my brother. And because I was suspected of having the welfare of the whole people also at heart (and what sovereign with a grain of wisdom could be otherwise minded?), I must be made to feel yet more severely that my kingdom was but the assured prey of these 'conquistadores.' (2)

After the *coup* had been completed, the plotters had the audacity to arrest the Queen and charge *her* with treason! About this charge, she had this to say:

> The substance of my crime was that I knew my people were conspiring to re-establish the constitutional government, to throw off the yoke of the stranger and

oppressor; and I had not conveyed this knowledge to the persons I had never recognized except as unlawful usurpers of authority, and had not informed against my own nation and against their friends who were also my long-time friends. (3)

The only charge against me really was that of being a queen; and my case was judged by these, my adversaries, before I came to court. I remember with clearness, however, the attack upon me by the Judge Advocate, the words issued from his mouth about 'the prisoner,' 'that woman,' etc., uttered with such affectation and disgust. The object of it was evidently to humiliate me, to make me break down in the presence of the staring crowd. But in this they were disappointed. My equanimity was never disturbed; and their own report relates that I throughout preserved 'that haughty carriage' which marked me as an 'unusual woman.' (4)

To that court she said, in part:

A minority of the foreign population made my action (consideration of a new constitution—author) the pretext for overthrowing the monarchy, and, aided by the United States naval forces and representative, established a new government.

I owed no allegiance to the Provisional Government so established, nor to any power or to any one save the will of my people and the welfare of my country.
The wishes of my people were not consulted as to this change in governments, and only those who were in practical rebellion against the constitutional government were allowed to vote upon the question whether the monarchy should exist or not. . . . (5)

These eloquent words, written in early 1895, along with others from her testimony, were deemed "offensive" by the court and ordered "stricken from the record." It would be hard to imagine a more obvious example of a criminal trying to cover his tracks.

Two years later, Lili'uokalani traveled to Washington to confer with the outgoing President, Grover Cleveland, who had treated her with dignity, respect, and justice. It will be instructive to see her writing in this regard.

> All the communications received, whether personally or in form, from individuals or from the above-named organizations, were in advocacy of one desired end. This was to ask President Cleveland that the former form of government unjustly taken from us by the persons who in 1892 and 1893 represented the United States should be restored, and that this restoration should undo the wrong which had been done to the Hawaiian people, and return to them the queen, to whom constitutionally, and also by their own choice, they had a perfect right.
>
> This was further in the line of the only instructions which to this day (1898—author) have ever been given by the United States to the so-called Republic of Hawaii, and those were that the President *acknowledges the right of the Hawaiian people to choose their own form of government.* (emphasis in the original) (6)

Speaking of the annexationist plotters, the Queen says they vacillate between calling themselves Americans and Hawaiians, depending upon which is to their advantage at any particular moment, pretending to represent Hawai'i at some points and at other times asserting their allegiance to the United States when it suited their schemes. She is very specific in detailing many by name, along with their personal history, calling them appropriately "pseudo-Hawaiians." She said as well, "At Honolulu these annexationists made speeches abusing the Senate of the United States for the delay in annexing Hawaii; they further said the most grossly insulting things of President Cleveland because he frustrated their plans . . ." (7).

After speaking of several examples of painful betrayal by people she had long known, she concludes her chapter on the pseudo-Hawaiians this way:

> Such has been the animosity, openly and secretly expressed, toward me not only as a queen, but as a woman, by those whom all the claims of gratitude should bind to me as friends, and who should rally to my assistance, that, since leaving home and arriving in America, I have often received communications from Hawaii, often by special message, begging me to be careful of my life, still regarded as 'infinitely precious to the people of the Islands,' reminding me that I was surrounded by enemies some of whom from home were entirely unscrupulous, and assuring me that great anxiety was felt by all classes, as it was a persistent rumor that evil was intended me. (8)

Being highly informed from many sources, very little escaped the Queen. She comments: "Thus, understanding perfectly the kind of men sent one after another by the so-called Republic of Hawaii to Washington, I was easily able to separate truth from falsehood in the accounts inspired by the missionary party, published by them or their agents in Honolulu, written from thence to the press in America, or invented by enterprising scribblers for the purpose of deceiving the American public." (9)

Upon being granted a visit to President Cleveland, the Queen says, after pleasantries pertaining to fond memories of Mrs. Cleveland who had been kind to the Queen:

> I handed him the documents prepared for his inspection by the patriotic leagues of which I have already spoken (these being the huge petitions containing signatures of thousands of Hawaiians rejecting annexation—author).
>
> These he took impressively, thanking me for them. It was a great pleasure to me to tell him personally how dear his name was to the Hawaiian people, and how grateful a place he held in my own heart because of his effort to do that which was right and just in restoring to us our lost independence. We always thought him to be sincere in his attempt to right the wrong; and since I have fully acquainted myself with the obstructions placed in his way by the supporters of Minister John L. Stevens, I understand far better than formerly that he failed through no fault of his own. (10)
>
> . . . I have never had the least cause to retract my early assurance that in Grover Cleveland I had met a statesman of splendid ability, rare judgment, and lofty standards of right. And equally do I believe that to few among the nations has it ever been granted to have at the head a woman more worthy the name of a queen than that one who presided with so much grace and dignity for eight years at the White House. (11)

There exist few people to whom the word "majesty" can truly apply, and still fewer who can enjoy that term in a justified manner while being head of state. Lili'uokalani was indeed one of those. Concluding this segment is one of the most dignified and subtle put-downs one can imagine. In her words:

> Strangers have remarked that in no part of the world visited by them have they found the rules of etiquette so exactly laid down and so persistently observed as in Honolulu, when the Islands were under the monarchy. It is to be expected, therefore that I know what is due me; that further, as the wife of the governor of Oahu, as the princess royal, and as reigning sovereign, it was not necessary for me to take lessons in the departments of social or diplomatic etiquette before residing in the national capital of the United States, or making and receiving visits of any nature. (12)

In the so-called Treaty of Annexation, which the Queen fought and unceasingly opposed, were provisions allegedly transferring sovereignty over the Hawaiian Islands to the United States. She correctly portrays this transfer as nothing more than an *empty quitclaim deed.* A quitclaim deed surrenders to the grantee only the interest in a property to which the grantor can lay claim in the first place. If the person has no ownership of a property, then obviously the deed is worthless. In her own example, the Queen says, "Any person could execute such a conveyance to the White House estate, and it would not convey anything, nor even pretend to put the grantee in possession of anything." (13) The most commonly used example in popular culture is a deed purporting to sell the Brooklyn Bridge. Quitclaim deeds have their place, as for example, when twenty people jointly own a piece of property, often from inheritance, and one party buys out shares of others, who then relinquish their (legitimate) claim in exchange for an agreed price. But as in the case of Hawai'i, those purporting to "convey" Hawai'i to the United States had no legitimate claim whatsoever other than their strident assertions.

Chapter 5

The Annexationist Plot and Hawaiian Resistance

In order to gain a full grasp of the rapidly evolving situation, it will be useful to examine the mindset of those responsible for the overthrow, for it is abundantly evident that the overthrow was regarded as a means to the end. That end was unquestionably annexation to the United States, even though some of the key participants had been, along with their parents, subjects of the nation of Hawai'i whose legitimate government was at the time headed by Queen Lili'uokalani.

The motivation and methodology of the annexationists was probably best laid out by the chief ideologist of this view at the time, Lorrin A. Thurston, publisher of the *Honolulu Advertiser,* still extant in merged form with its longtime rival the *Honolulu Star-Bulletin* and which remained in the family well into the second half of the 20th century. In his booklet *Handbook on the Annexation of Hawaii,* published in 1897, Thurston laid out methodically the reasons he saw for this change in political status.

His primary reason, as being an advantage to the U.S. strategic position globally, was that Hawai'i is located in the center of the huge Pacific Ocean with thousands of miles of ocean in every direction, so as to serve as an ideal staging and refueling area. By denying Hawai'i to any other country, he reasoned, would ensure the safety of the West Coast of the U.S. from attack. Furthermore, with the planned completion of the "Nicaragua or Panama Canal" (anticipated but not yet begun), Hawaii would make an ideal stopping point for fuel and supplies for ships going to and from Asia. (1)

Thurston's second point is related to the first. Anticipating the continued downward trend of Native

Hawaiians in population, he projected a time when either a foreign power would make a grab for Hawai'i or the U.S. would do so. In essence he called for a preemptive first strike to seize Hawai'i. (2)The morality of seizing the land and sovereignty of an independent nation did not seem to appear in the equation at all. He sounds to this author like a political ancestor of Nixon's Secretary of State, who, by inference, gave the approval to Indonesia's plan to overrun East Timor with no concern for the human rights of the native people, and his dismissal of concerns for the fate of Micronesians living on their tiny islands not being a factor when considering U.S. global strategic objectives.

He further reasoned that as long as Hawai'i was sovereign, it had the power to make and cancel treaties with any nation it pleased, perhaps to the detriment of the United States. In this regard he raised presciently the specter of an awakening Japan and the (to him) alarming number of Japanese laborers imported to work on the plantations, with implications of continued loyalty to Japan. In this regard he cited an 1896 census that stated that there were at the time more adult men of Japanese ancestry than of any other nationality, and went on to project numbers based on such a rate of influx. (3)

Even though they (then currently) had no right to vote, it would be foreseeable that legislation would eventually pass to allow it, with implications regarding ultimate national loyalty. (4) Thurston boldly states,

> The issue in Hawaii is not between monarchy and the Republic. That issue has been settled. There are some persons who do not recognize this fact. There are never lacking those who set their faces backward; who mourn every lost cause and vainly hope for the restoration of abused and forfeited power.

> *The present Hawaiian-Japanese controversy is the preliminary skirmish in the great coming struggle between the civilization and the awakening forces of the East and the civilization of the West.* (5) (emphasis in the original).

It must be noted that even Thurston must acknowledge that Hawai'i is a country, not a colony, not a territory, not vacant land. "The population of the country is so small that individual influence is much greater than in a larger country, and it is much easier for a nationality or a faction to get control of the government.

"As long as the country is independent, with its growing wealth and importance there is, and will be, a growing tendency to internationalize friction among its inhabitants, which will inevitably draw into controversy the respective governments. . . .

"Hawaii independent, but without the power to maintain its independence, is a standing invitation to international intrigue and friction, and a menace to the peace of the Pacific." (6)

It was very convenient to place the blame for potential war on the desire of Hawaiians to be independent, rather than on potentially aggressive actions taken by imperial powers, sort of like blaming 1930s Czechoslovakia for being small and "inviting" Germany to invade. This type of reasoning has its echoes in today's political pronouncements as well, except that today's claims generally have to do with the words "weapons of mass destruction" from the country which has the lion's share of them.

In contrast to the self-serving commentary on the "inevitability" of the termination of sovereignty, Thurston cites the 1896 population census, which I have no reason to doubt, except that it may under-represent Native Hawaiians, since some lived in remote areas not readily accessible. The numbers are rounded for convenience in his citation:

Total population is 109,020	
Native Hawaiians	31,000
Japanese	24,400
Portuguese	15,100
Chinese	21,600
Part Hawaiian and part foreign blood	8,400
Americans	3,000
British	2,200
German	1,400
Norwegian and French	479
All other nationalities	1,055 (7)

The degree to which the perspective of history can be altered by the slant of the narrator can easily be seen in Thurston's summary description under his heading "Form of Government."

> The government of Hawaii was a monarchy until January, 1893, when Queen Liliuokalani attempted to abrogate the constitution and promulgate one increasing her power and disenfranchising the whites.
>
> The people thereupon overthrew the monarchy and established a Provisional Government, January the 17th, 1893.
>
> Later a constitutional convention unanimously adopted a constitution declaring the Republic of Hawaii, on July 4, 1894. . . .
>
> THE ELECTORATE (capitals in original) consists of all male adult citizens who take an oath of renunciation of the monarchy and allegiance to the Republic. *Asiatics are not eligible to citizenship or to vote.* (italics in original) (8)

Several major distortions occur here. To begin with, the Queen's subjects, in large numbers, implored her to reject the imposed "bayonet constitution" of 1887 because it had disenfranchised them in major ways. Under it, and the one the Queen would have proposed consistent with it, white aliens (but not Asian aliens) and Hawaiian subjects all had equal votes. However, white aliens were badly outnumbered. This is not "disenfranchisement;" this is what is called "democracy."

Further, as we have seen, it was not "the people" who overthrew the Queen, but a tiny group of ambitious whites (not all Americans) following the ideology of Mr. Thurston along with the complicity of the U.S. Minister Stevens and the commanding officer of the warship Boston with its armed troops who conducted the overthrow.

Thurston, an adept writer, turns "devil's advocate" and answers some of the real or anticipated objections to his plan for annexation to the United States. It will be useful to look at a few of them.

Objection: *Whether the annexation of a non-homogenous people is constitutional or not, the population of Hawaii is unfit for incorporation into, and will be dangerous to the American political system.* (9) (Italics in original)

Thurston's response was to point out that Hawai'i's legal system is based on English law and that it varies only about as much as law differs from one state to another, and that English is the language of education. Furthermore, "The people of Hawaii as a whole, are energetic and industrious. They are annually producing and exporting more per capita than any other nation in the world." Such industrious production indicates the people are not "lazy, worthless, or unreliable. . . .As a matter of fact, there are no poor houses, beggars, or tramps in Hawaii." (10)

Continuing his answer to his own question, he added that Hawaiians are "conservative, peaceful, and generous." His next statement, however, is extraordinary in how badly it characterized Hawaiian sentiment toward the subject of annexation. . . ."a very large proportion of them . . .are supporters of the Republic and of annexation." (11) To call this wishful thinking on Thurston's part would be a tactful and generous way of characterizing this viewpoint.

Thurston, seeking to appease racist sentiment in the U.S., states further,

> The Hawaiians are not Africans, but Polynesians. They are brown, not black. There is not, and never has been any color line in Hawaii as against native Hawaiians, and they participate fully and on an equality with the white people in affairs political, social, religious and charitable. The two races freely intermarry one with the other, the results being shown in a present population of some 7000 of mixed blood. (12)
>
> THE CHINESE AND JAPANESE (capitals in original) are an undesirable population from a political standpoint. . . .As soon as they accumulate a few hundred dollars they return home. . . . Individually, the Chinese and Japanese in Hawaii are industrious, peaceable citizens, and as long as they do not take part in the political control of the country, what danger can the comparatively small number there be to this country? (13)

Another objection Thurston raised, and then answered, from his perspective is the following: *A large portion of the Hawaiian voters have been disenfranchised: No vote has been taken in Hawaii upon the question of annexation and it is un-American to annex a territory without a popular vote of its inhabitants..* . . . (italics in original)

Whether it is un-American to annex territory without a popular vote, depends upon what has been done on like occasions in the past. In the cases of the annexation of Louisiana, with its colony of intelligent Frenchmen; of Florida, with its Spaniards; of California, New Mexico, Arizona, and Alaska, there was no semblance of a vote, and there is no indication that the subject was so much as discussed by either of the contracting parties. All that was done or lawfully required to be done, was the agreement of the two Governments and the act was complete without reference to either the people of the United States or of the territory proposed to be annexed. . . . .

There is less reason for taking a popular vote in the case of Hawaii than in any instance in the past, for the reason that there is not now and never has been any Hawaiian law requiring that a treaty of annexation should be submitted to a popular vote; but, on the contrary, there is specifically incorporated into the Constitution of the Republic an article authorizing and directing the President, by and with the consent of the Senate, to negotiate and conclude a treaty of annexation with the United States.

Again, why in logic is there any more reason for requiring a popular vote on the part of the citizens of Hawaii than by the citizens of the United States? The citizens of the United States, as well as those of Hawaii assume responsibilities and obligations by reason of annexation. Why should the citizens of Hawaii be individually consulted, and those of the United States ignored?

Incidentally, however, as in the case of Texas, there has been a practical vote in Hawaii upon the subject of annexation, for every person who is now a voter in

> Hawaii has taken the oath to the Constitution of Hawaii, thereby ratifying and approving of annexation to the United States.. . .
>
> The only persons who could vote under the monarchy and who cannot vote now, are those who have disenfranchised themselves by refusing to accept the Republic. . . . Unless annexation takes place, the only future for the native Hawaiian is retrogression to the status of the Asiatic coolie, who is already crowding him to the wall. (14)

Where does one begin to analyze such self-serving convoluted statements? The U.S. Declaration of Independence correctly and wisely states that the *legitimacy* of a government derives from the *consent of the governed.* Thurston conveniently disregards this bedrock of U.S. history.

In the case of Hawai'i, a *fully developed national government,* recognized as such from the 1840s the world over, including the United States, had been in existence for close to a hundred years prior to the *coup d'etat* that overthrew the monarchy. Moreover, abundant evidence exists that the overwhelming majority of the people of Hawai'i were content with their government, and it had their consent, unlike the fraudulent "Republic of Hawaii."

As for the argument that there was no law requiring a vote in the case of annexation, that would be like saying there is no law requiring a vote of the people of the U.S. if China (for instance) decided to annex this country! Why should it even come up? Further, it is profoundly dishonest to say that every voter in Hawai'i had taken an oath to support the (newly imposed) Constitution that included a provision that asked for such an annexation. People were not allowed to vote *unless* they agreed to such terms! It disregards the fact that the makers of the *coup d'etat* were the same ones who invented the "Provisional Government" which in President Grover Cleveland's view was neither *de facto* nor *de jure.* That is to say, as merely a self-proclaimed committee without popular support outside a handful of plotters, it had no legitimacy to rule, much less to act on behalf of the people of Hawai'i (of *all* nationalities) to request annexation. Specifically, Thurston refused to address the overwhelming majority of Hawaiian subjects, including some ethnic non-Hawaiians, who were outraged by the idea of burglarized sovereignty, pretending dishonestly that this sentiment did not exist. Finally, in one last fit of racist arrogance, he declared without merit that the only other option would be submergence under a wave of Asian influence, described negatively. Furthermore, Thurston disregards the legitimate treaties entered into by the monarchy with numerous established independent countries, as previously cited.

Alarmed by such prospects, Hawaiians, under the leadership of the beloved deposed Queen, organized resistance on a massive but remarkably peaceful scale. References to resistance appeared in various writings of the time, but the *extent of this resistance* was not understood in the contemporary time of renaissance (1970 onward) until a Hawaiian woman researcher named Noenoe Silva took her clues (assorted references) to the United States Library of Congress and located the mother lode of protest in 1995, ninety-eight years later. She brought to public attention the original petitions signed by tens of thousands of Native Hawaiians along with some non-Hawaiians who decried the loss of sovereignty proposed by annexation. This appeared to be a gigantic effort, for within a matter of weeks, petitioners fanned out to distant reaches of the islands, and a total of 21,269 signatures were collected in the fall of 1897.

This effort was accomplished through two parallel organizations, Hui Aloha 'Aina o Na Kane (for men) and Hui Aloha 'Aina o Na Wahine (for women). Hui Aloha Aina can be roughly translated as "organization for love of the land." In Silva's words, in this context, the phrase meant "loyal

Kanaka Maoli—a patriot." While these petitions explicitly and emphatically rejected annexation as the sole issue, another organization, Hui Kalai'aina circulated a separate petition drive to restore the monarchy in numbers of approximately 17,000, no doubt overlapping with the anti-annexation petitioners. (15)

Recognizing the urgency of the matter, a delegation of four was sent to Washington, D.C. in December 1897, meeting first with Queen Lili'uokalani, who was there already. "Together, they decided to present the petitions of Hui Aloha 'Aina only, because Hui Aloha Aina's was a 'petition protesting annexation,' while Hui Kalai'aina's petition called for the restoration of the monarchy. They agreed that they did not want to appear divided." (16)

Replicas of this mass of signatures were returned to Hawai'i within a year of their discovery (1995) and were displayed at the Bishop Museum, a major center for preserving artifacts and for scholarship not only of Hawai'i but other Polynesian peoples, located in Honolulu. This display was observed by this writer, who was impressed by large walls covered in full by the names of these thousands of sincere people, determined that their rights of self determination should not remain violated. The exhibit was electrifying for many Hawaiians who discovered that in almost every case they could find an ancestor who had signed the petitions, and this became a major source of pride that their ancestors had not, after all, rolled over and accepted annexation passively. This history of protest had been lost for just under 100 years.

Notwithstanding the peaceful, rational, legal, yet vehement petition protest and the sympathetic agreement by many prominent Americans who objected to the blatant absence of common decency and fair play, the outbreak of the Spanish American War at just this time in history (1898), together with obvious jingoistic journalism, led to a chauvinistic land grab consistent with the views of the new president, William McKinley, succeeding Grover Cleveland. Among the lands seized during a brief period were (besides Hawai'i) Philippines, Guam, Puerto Rico, and Cuba. Practically overnight, the United States ceased to be a nation and became an empire, which today has military forces stationed in over one hundred countries.

During these frantic times, international law and the numerous valid treaties between the Kingdom of Hawai'i and other countries, including the United States, were simply ignored and violated. In reality, a state of war existed between the United States and Spain, with Hawai'i being a neutral party, by international law. Naturally, the military position was that they "needed Hawai'i" both for their own staging purposes and even more importantly, to deny Hawai'i's resources to any other country, most notably, Spain. These violations of international law, namely the disregard of existing valid treaties entered into with good faith on both sides prior to the 1890s' mischief, are still pending international review.

Upon the taking of office by William McKinley as president of the United States, a new effort was made to achieve annexation, which the Queen bravely and eloquently opposed. She appealed to the Senate of the United States, whose two-thirds vote was required to confirm a treaty of annexation. Her appeal was signed June 17, 1897. It states, in part:

> I, Liliuokalani of Hawaii, by the will of God named heir apparent on the tenth day of April, AD 1877, and by the grace of God Queen of the Hawaiian Islands on the seventeenth day of January AD 1893, do hereby protest against the ratification of a certain treaty, which, so I am informed, has been signed at Washington by Mssrs. Hatch, Thurston, and Kinney, purporting to cede those islands to the territory and

dominion of the United States. I declare such a treaty to be an act of wrong toward the native and part-native people of Hawaii, and invasion of the rights of the ruling chiefs, in violation of international rights both toward my people and toward friendly nations with whom they have made treaties, the perpetuation of the fraud whereby the constitutional government was overthrown, and finally, an act of gross injustice to me. . .

Because the President of the United States, the Secretary of State, and an envoy commissioned by them reported in official documents that my government was unlawfully coerced by the forces, diplomatic and naval, of the United States; that I was at the date of their investigations the constitutional ruler of my people. . . .

Because neither the above-named commission nor the government which sends it has ever received any such authority from the registered voters of Hawaii, but derives its assumed powers from the so-called committee of public safety, organized on or about the seventeenth day of January, 1893, said committee being composed largely of persons claiming American citizenship, and not one single Hawaiian was a member thereof, or in any way participated in the demonstration leading to its existence.

Because my people, about forty thousand in number, have in no way been consulted by those, three thousand in number, who claim the right to destroy the independence of Hawaii. My people constitute four fifths of the legally qualified voters of Hawaii, and excluding those imported for the demands of labor, about the same proportion of the inhabitants.

CIVIC AND HEREDITARY RIGHTS

Because said treaty ignores, not only the civic rights of my people, but, further, their hereditary property of their chiefs. Of the 4,000,000 acres comprising the territory said treaty offers to annex, 1,000,000 or 915,000 acres has in no way been heretofore recognized as other than the private property of the constitutional monarch, subject to a control in no way differing from other items of a private estate.

Because said treaty ignores, not only all professions of perpetual amity and good faith made by the United States in former treaties with the sovereigns representing the Hawaiian people, but all treaties made by those sovereigns with other and friendly powers, and it is thereby in violation of international law.

Because, by treating with the parties claiming at this time the right to cede said territory of Hawaii, the Government of the United States receives such territory from the hands of those whom its own magistrates (legally elected by the people of the United States, and in office in 1893) pronounced fraudulently in power and unconstitutionally ruling Hawaii.

APPEALS TO PRESIDENT AND SENATE

Therefore I, Liliuokalani of Hawaii, do hereby call upon the President of that nation, to whom alone I yielded my property and authority, to withdraw said treaty (ceding said Islands) from further consideration. I ask the honorable Senate of the United States to decline to ratify said treaty, and I implore the people of this great and good nation, from whom my ancestors learned the

> Christian religion, to sustain their representatives in such acts of justice and equity as may be in accord with the principles of their fathers, and to the Almighty Ruler of the universe, to him who judgeth righteously, I commit my cause. (17)

Commenting on the treaty and the treachery involved in perpetrating it, the Queen comments further:

> It is not for me to consider this matter from the American point of view; although the pending question of annexation involves nothing less that a departure from the established policy of that country, and an ominous change in its foreign relations. It is enough that I am able to say, and with absolute authority, that the native people of Hawaii are entirely faithful to their own chiefs, and are deeply attached to their own customs and mode of government; that they either do not understand, or bitterly oppose, the scheme of annexation. As a native Hawaiian, reared and educated in close intimacy with the present rulers of the Islands and their families, with exceptional opportunities for studying both native and foreign character, it is easy for me to detect the purpose of each line and word in the annexation treaty, and even to distinguish the man originating each portion of it. (18)

Submitted through appropriate diplomatic channels at that time as well were the petition signatures of tens of thousands of people from Hawaii, referenced earlier, adamantly opposing annexation and in support of their Queen. President McKinley, whose sympathies were conspicuously with the annexationists, disregarded this massive and cogent protest and submitted the annexation treaty to the Senate, where it failed to obtain the two-thirds support necessary for passage. This failure was due in large measure to the heroic efforts of the Hawaiian patriots under the leadership of the intelligent and widely respected Queen. But the resultant jubilation among Hawaii's citizens was short-lived.

In preparation for the impending "annexation," a mere two months before the fraud was committed, Captain Alfred T. Mahan testified on May 10, 1898 before Congress:

> It is obvious that if we do not hold the islands ourselves we can not expect the neutrals in the war to prevent the other belligerent (implying Spain—author) from occupying them; nor can the inhabitants themselves prevent such occupation. The commercial value is not great enough to provoke neutral interposition. In short, in war we should need a larger Navy to defend the Pacific coast, because we should have not only to defend our coast, but to prevent, by naval force, an enemy from occupying the islands; whereas, if we *pre-occupied* them, fortifications could preserve them to us. In my opinion it is not practicable for any trans-Pacific country to invade our Pacific coast without *occupying* Hawai'i as a base. (emphasis added by author of the Dominion book) (19)

U.S. Army General John Schofield added:

> We got a preemption title to those islands through the volunteer action of our American missionaries who went there and civilized and Christianized those people and established a Government that has no parallel in the history of the world, considering its age, and we made a preemption which nobody in the world thinks of disputing, provided we perfect our title. *If we do not perfect it in due time, we have lost those islands.* (emphasis added by *Dominion* author) (20)

Note that he gives credit for the formation of a modern, democratic, civilized government, not to the Hawaiian majority but to the missionaries, the descendants of whom were among the very conspirators who were responsible for its overthrow. It is a measure of the racism of the time that neither of these statements acknowledged the clear viewpoints of the Hawaiian majority that in fact **did dispute** just such a preemption, a racist neglect of the vital "consent of the governed" that had its echo 65 years later in Vietnam, as well as other countries, notably in Central and South America, during the 20th century.

Unable to secure passage of a treaty between the United States and the fraudulent "Republic of Hawaii," the annexationists succeeded in barely passing a "Joint Resolution of Congress" to annex Hawai'i, needing only 50% plus one for passage. "Thus, the purported sovereignty of the self-proclaimed Republic of Hawai'i, *and not the sovereignty of the Hawaiian Kingdom* (emphasis added by this author) were transferred to the United States of America. On a platform at the base of Iolani Palace in Honolulu, Harold Sewall, from the McKinley administration and successor to United States Minister Willis of the Cleveland administration, stated:

> 'Mr. President (Note: Sanford B. Dole of the Republic of Hawai'i—author), I present you a certified copy of a joint resolution of the Congress of the United States, approved by the President on July 7th, 1898, entitled "Joint Resolution to provide for annexing the Hawaiian Islands to the United States" This joint resolution accepts, ratifies, and confirms, on the part of the United States, the cession formally consented to and approved by the Republic of Hawai'i.' " (21)

The reader may recall the early passage of this book wherein the absurd scenario was presented in which the Congress of the United States had voted to "annex"

Denmark. Whether we use Denmark, Peru, Thailand, or any other country, the procedure is entirely without legal merit—likewise with Hawai'i in 1898. Who would give any credence to an act of the California Legislature declaring that Nevada was "annexed" and that all Nevadan laws were summarily cancelled, that Nevada was now subject to all existing California laws? To make an even more ridiculous claim, since Nevada is contiguous with California, let us propose that the same Legislature declared that Tennessee was instantly "annexed" (since the distance from Tennessee is roughly the same to California as California is to Hawai'i). Clearly the jurisdiction of the legislating party would have been exceeded, just as it was in the case of Hawai'i in 1898.

Sanford B. Dole, a willing participant in this legal charade, replied on behalf of the self-proclaimed "Republic of Hawai'i":

> A treaty (sic.—author) of political union having been made, and the cession formally consented to and approved by the Republic of Hawai'i, having been accepted by the United States of America, I now, in the interest of the Hawaiian body politic, and with full confidence in the honor, justice and friendship of the American people, yield up to you as the representative of the Government of the United States, the sovereignty and public property of the Hawaiian Islands. (22)

As we can now see, the legal effect of such a granting of sovereignty is the same as if you signed over all your right, title, and interest to the Brooklyn Bridge!

In early 1900, Congress passed a law providing for a government for the "Territory of Hawai'i" which amounted to a puppet regime, which of course continued to ignore the matter of the disenfranchisement of the overwhelming majority of the people. The governor was appointed by the U.S. president, not elected. The people of Hawai'i, without their consent, were classified as United States citizens and citizens of the Territory of Hawai'i. (23) Imagine the psychological impact of national identity theft! Suppose for example, that in some future time, the U.S. was weak and subject to just such encroachments and U.S. citizens awoke to the news, due to intrigues at the highest level, that they are henceforth to be citizens of Brazil, Japan, China, or Russia!

Chapter 6

Occupation

From 1900 onward for the next half century and more, the people of Hawai'i and especially Native Hawaiians, were treated much like what we call today "a third world country." Hawai'i saw continual encroachment—militarily, economically, politically, and socially. Its resources continued to be plundered, and Hawaiian people were repressed, not often in a brutal manner, like massacres, but severely, as in control of all directions.

Like Native American peoples, Hawaiian children were forbidden to use their own language and punished when they did. Teachers sometimes went so far as to visit the homes and lecture Hawaiian speaking parents on the need to use English. Hawaiians of all ages were coerced into being obedient English-speaking Christian "American citizens," and in the interests of personal survival, most complied. Hawaiian religion and legacy of music were discouraged. Resistance went underground. One testimony to such resistance is the song *Kaulana Na Pua*, familiar today to anyone reasonably appreciative of Hawaiian music. Written in 1898, it expressed the outrage of loss of sovereignty and determination to resist. The words go like this:

Kaulana na pua a'o Hawai'i
Kupa'a mahope o ka aina
Hiki mai ka'elele o ka loko'ino
Palapala anunu me ka pahaka

Jon Olsen

Pane mai Hawai'i moku o Keawe
Kokua no hono a'o Pi'ilani
Kako'o mai Kaua'i o mano
Pa'apu me ke one Kakuhihewa

'A'ole makou a'e minamina
I ka pu'ukala a ke aupuni
Ua lawa makou i ka pohaku
I ka'ai kamaha'o o ka 'aina

Ma hope makou o Lili'ulani
A loa'a 'e ka pono a ka 'aina
*(A kau hou 'ia e ke kalaunu)
Ha'ina 'ia mai ana ka puana
Ka po'e i ahoha i ka 'aina
*(alternate stanza)

In English:

Famous are the children of Hawai'i
Ever loyal to the land
When the evil-hearted messenger comes
With his greedy document of extortion

Hawai'i, land of Keawe answers
Pi'ilani's bays help
Mano's Kaua'i lends support
And so do the sands of Kakuhikewa

No one will fix a signature
To the paper of the enemy
With its sin of annexation
And sale of native civil rights

We do not value
The government's sums of money
We are satisfied with the stones
Astonishing food of the land

We back Lili'olani
Who has won the rights of the land
*(She will be crowned again)
Tell the story
Of the people who love their land
*(Alternate stanza)

At the ceremony that allegedly transferred sovereignty to the United States, the delight evident in the mood of the annexationists was matched by the visible grief of Hawaiians. "Invited to play, the Royal Hawaiian Band did not come, while the Hawaiians in the National Guard covered their faces as the stars and stripes were hoisted up the pole. According to one observer, Rear Admiral L.A. Beardslee, 'The band of Hawaiian damsels who were to have lowered for the last time the Hawaiian flag would not lower it. The band refused to play the *ponoi* (the Hawaiian national anthem—author) and loud weeping was the only music contributed by the natives.' While congressmen and military officers attended a splendidly catered annexationist ball and danced with *haole* debutantes in long white dresses, the *Advertiser* trumpeted: 'HAWAII BECOMES THE FIRST OUTPOST OF A GREATER AMERICA.' " (1)

Almost immediately following the alleged annexation, a rapid influx of capital and new technology flowed into Hawai'i, including a trans-Pacific cable that permitted telephone communication to and from the mainland U.S. and proliferation of electrical usage. The Caucasian elite of Hawai'i simultaneously increased their power within the island community and their integration into the American capitalist system. Nearly every economic enterprise fell under

The Big Five (as the major Hawai'i-based corporations were called), and later Dillingham Corporation as well: shipping, banking, insurance, plantations, construction, wholesale and retail operations, and so on, with island-based interlocking directorates from among the dominant wealthy Caucasian families, names familiar to all who have lived long in Hawai'i: Bishop, Castle, Cooke, Brewer, Davies, Dole, Atherton, Damon, Baldwin, Robinson, Dillingham. To give an example, one man, E.D. Tenney, headed simultaneously, Castle and Cooke, Matson Navigation, Hawaiian Trust Company and three plantations, while sitting on the board of directors of twelve other companies! (2)

Walter F. Dillingham entered the fray from a different angle, by cultivating U.S. military authorities in Washington, and in the process obtained contracts for numerous military construction projects in Hawai'i over decades. (3)

Feudal-like economic control led directly to feudal-like political control during the first forty-five years of the 20th century. "Legislative bills were drawn up in downtown offices of corporate attorneys and transmitted to corporate controlled politicians at Iolani Palace." (4) "Public land" (not conceding here the theft perpetrated by alleged annexation) was seized by plantations for as little as 2 cents per acre per year! (5)

Innumerable examples could be provided about the virtual stranglehold of the Hawaiian economy by the Big Five plus Dillingham, the interlocking families by marriage, and interlocking corporate directorships. By such complete dominance, and the fact that no one could simply truck products across from another state, as one can on the mainland, due to a separation of 2500 miles of ocean, these corporate giants were able to charge exorbitant prices and generate bloated profit margins for decades. Only in very recent times, say 1980 to the present, with the influx of "big box" stores have prices begun to approach those that exist for mainland customers for the same products. But this trend is certainly a mixed blessing, for this presence, as on the mainland, has driven out small local businesses that had survived on the periphery of the Big Five by carving out niche markets and providing good "aloha-style" service.

Leery of the large numbers of Japanese by the time of "annexation," the large plantation owners began to import Filipino workers by the thousands, and later Koreans. Plantations developed living camps, organized by ethnicity. Pay for identical work was not equal, in order to consciously create divisions and petty jealousies among workers.

Typical of ruling classes, the elite of Hawai'i used both carrot and stick. They did provide a low level standard of housing, medical care, and recreational facilities, all the better to contain potential ambitions to leave.

Coercion was the other side of the coin. "Nine decades of playing race against race, of beatings, shootings, blacklists, and myriad forms of brutalization are summarized in a terse 1939 statement by the U.S. Department of Labor: 'Hawaiian management has used every influence at its command to restrict labor organizing.' " (6) Further, "The commissioner of labor statistics reported in 1916 that the planters "view laborers primarily as instruments of production, their business interests require cheap, not too intelligent, docile unmarried men." (7)

One of the permanent laws of social interaction states that "Where there is oppression, there will be resistance." Why should it be otherwise in Hawai'i? Between 1920 and 1940 there were several attempts to organize labor by ethnicity with major strikes, which were put down by a combination of corporate law and corporate-directed police repression. In a few cases workers were actually shot and killed by police in service to their corporate masters. Various commentators compared the social climate in Hawai'i at this time (1930s) to fascism and to old southern U.S. slavery.

Then came World War II. It came to Hawai'i suddenly early one Sunday morning on a day the world will long remember: December 7, 1941. Pearl Harbor, a magnificent natural harbor, one of the major reasons for the "annexation," roughly eight miles from downtown Honolulu, was bombed severely by Japanese planes coming from aircraft carriers. Citizens of Hawai'i of Japanese ancestry were immediately suspect, but because of their numbers and significance in the local economy, they were not subject to the same wholesale roundup and discrimination as Japanese on the mainland U.S. faced. In view of the need for national unity while facing two formidable foes, labor leaders entered a truce period with the oppressive employers. Martial law was imposed. Since WW II has been written about extensively, this work will pass over it lightly.

During the early course of the war, the entire island of Kaho'olawe was seized for use by the U. S. military. Lightly populated at the time, and consisting of some forty-five square miles and used primarily for ranching, it was used for the next half century as a munitions target, particularly by aircraft using bombs. In later decades, other nations were also invited by military authorities to engage in "joint exercises" which compounded the original antagonism experienced by Hawaiians. In the mid 1970's the sight of the island, struggling to remain a viable place to sustain life, fired the emotions of many Hawaiians, especially those on the islands closest to Kaho'olawe, namely Maui and Moloka'i, from which the sights and sounds of the bombing raids were clearly visible and audible. This island became one of the most important areas of contention between Native Hawaiians and the military forces of the United States. In that process, the modern sovereignty movement began.

Shortly after the end of WW II, in conjunction with the return of large numbers of former plantation workers turned soldiers, the labor movement picked up in earnest, led primarily by the International Longshoremen's and Warehousemen's Union (ILWU) Local 142, under the local leadership of Jack Hall, and by extension, Harry Bridges on the mainland. What the ILWU was able to achieve after the war, which had not been done prior to it, was to organize workers *across ethnic lines* so that the employing class were not able to use their standard ethnic divide and conquer methods. Included in the new big union were not only the dock workers (from whom came the name of the union) but also workers on both sugar and pineapple plantations on all islands.

A half century of virtual total control by industry management and its political allies came into direct conflict with the newly organized and rapidly growing ILWU on Sept. 1, 1946 when over fifteen thousand sugar workers, unified across lines of nationality, went on strike for better wages, union security, and most fundamentally, respect. The strike lasted until Nov. 18, 1946, with the union winning significant gains, including a near doubling of the base pay.

This strike was followed the next year by one in the pineapple industry, but it was more of a draw due to tactical errors on the union side. Then in 1949 came the big longshore strike, based largely on the issue of wage parity with the West Coast dock workers. The strike began on May Day. This was the era of rabid red-baiting as well, which came into play through the media, which of course was dominated then, as now, by an employer perspective. The strike lasted 177 days and had a huge impact far beyond the immediate players, since it disrupted normal commerce on a broad scale causing belt-tightening across the board. By the end of the strike, some 17.6 percent of the work force were unemployed. The strike resulted in a modest financial gain for the workers but more importantly, they had broken the power of the shipping and commercial class to dictate terms without reprisal. The scale tipped a little further in the direction of labor. (8).

Political change came in 1954, a year sometimes called the "1954 Revolution," rather a misnomer but truly a moment of historical change. That year a coalition was built which undid 50 years of rule by the Republican oligarchy.

This newly enfranchised and united labor force combined with political liberals eager for social reform, and returning veterans of WW II, large numbers of whom were Japanese who had fought valiantly in Europe and who were absolutely not going to return to the semi-feudal conditions they had left behind. These forces consolidated the rule of Democrats in 1954 and remained the dominant party for another nearly fifty years.

However, being the party in power brings temptations of abuse of power and financial deals "under the table." Though rarely proven, such suspicions, particularly with regard to government contracts and political contributions, have undermined trust of Democrats in Hawai'i. As a result, a Republican, Linda Lingle, was elected in 2002, the first Republican governor since the 1950s.

Chapter 7

The Allegation of "Statehood"

Certainly the vast majority of readers will assert, "Wasn't the matter of Hawai'i's status settled once and for all by the vote for statehood in 1959?" After all, for over fifty years now we have been told Hawai'i is the 50th state, and there are 50 stars in the flag to prove it! Before we look at the evidence, I will remind the reader that political boundaries change more frequently than do the beds of rivers, but even the latter can change as a result of earthquakes and volcanoes. In particular, as we have seen many times in the 20th century, colonies become independent nations, empires fragment, new alignments occur. Permanency is an illusion, one fostered by rulers to keep subjects in line.

Hawai'i, as a "territory of the United States," (sic) held a plebiscite in conjunction with an election in Hawaii on June 27, 1959, asking the question "Shall Hawai'i immediately be admitted into the Union as a State?" Not surprisingly, after half a century of intense Americanization which negated education about the history of the overthrow and annexation, except to exalt the latter, and considering that the Native Hawaiian population continued to decline and become demoralized, the vote was for approval. The *only other option allowed was to remain in the inferior position of "territory," a quasi-colony.* So thorough had been the indoctrination that even progressive people looked at statehood as an advance (now we get representation in Washington, D.C.!) rather than a retreat. This act of "statehood" constituted another sleight-of-hand by the U.S., the first being the pretense that the "Republic of Hawai'i" represented anything more than a handful of *coup* plotters. Based on this "induced vote," President Eisenhower proclaimed on August 21, 1959 that

Hawai'i was henceforth a state equal to all the others. (1) Here's how they played the international game in 1959. As a charter member of the United Nations, the U.S. was bound by the terms of the Charter, which among other things proclaimed "a process of de-colonization for those people who have *not yet attained* independence as a nation." (emphasis in original) (2) This process is in direct support of the internationally recognized value stated in General Assembly Resolution 1514 that ". . '.all peoples have the right to self-determination; by virtue of that right they freely determine their political status and freely pursue their economic, social and cultural development.' " (3)

The outright fraud and sleight-of-hand occurred as the U.S. attempted to include "the Hawaiian Islands as a U.S. colony along with Alaska, American Samoa, Guam, Panama Canal Zone, Puerto Rico and the Virgin Islands. The underlying problem here was that the Hawaiian Kingdom had already achieved independence for the Hawaiian Islands since 1842, and the United States and other members of the Community of States also recognized this independence." So, the issue was moot and the vote was of no legal consequence. None of the others included in the list had achieved such international status. (4) But due to this "new status" as a state, the U.S. declared that it no longer was bound to report to the UN about Hawai'i. (5)

So what is the legal case for a rejuvenation of true sovereignty as an independent nation of Hawai'i? Recall that annexation may be achieved through a mutually agreed treaty of annexation at the executive level between the "annexor" and the "annexee." In the case of Hawai'i, the imaginary annexation took place through an act of Congress, **which has legal power only within the United States.** That is, Congress can only impose its laws within the domain of the United States, not within any foreign country, whether Canada, France, or Hawai'i in 1898.This dilemma was referenced obliquely in 1988 by Douglas W. Kmiec, Acting

Assistant U.S. Attorney General, in reference to a matter of extending authority further into the ocean: "There is a serious question whether Congress has the authority either to assert jurisdiction over an expanded territorial sea for purposes of international law or to assert the United States' sovereignty over it." More significantly, **"It is therefore unclear which Constitutional power Congress exercised when it acquired Hawai'i by joint resolution."** (emphasis added by this author) (6). One could add, "If they had any authority at all!"

If the transfer of power from the "Republic of Hawai'i" (which was a usurper non-legitimate government, as acknowledged explicitly by then sitting President Grover Cleveland), was also illegitimate, then the nation of Hawai'i **never became** a "U.S. Territory" and the 1959 Statehood Act and subsequent U.S. sponsored "plebiscite" was likewise illegitimate, and ought to be considered null and void. In effect, this scenario can be legitimately called a triple sleight-of-hand worthy or the most skilled magician: (a) the *coup* against the Queen, during which she surrendered both temporarily and conditionally to the United States in view of its overwhelming military power in order to save lives, after which the plotters acted *as if* she had surrendered unconditionally, (b) the pretended annexation and subsequent setting up of a "Territorial Government," contrary to both international law and to the expressed wished of the great majority of the people of Hawai'i, and finally (c) the fraudulent "statehood" fiasco. If this were a chess match, advocates of full Hawaiian sovereignty would have achieved checkmate. **The U.S. position is legally absolutely untenable.** Only by way of military occupation and subsequent diplomatic bluster can the United States to this day maintain the *status quo*.

What do scholars of international law have to say that is relevant to the matter? Several direct quotations should suffice to clinch the argument. The first is by Prof. K. Marek in a 1968 article entitled *Idcntity and Continuity in Public*

International Law:

> . . .whether a law-breaking attitude of the occupying power makes it possible for the legal order of the occupied State to retain a certain amount of effectiveness in the occupied territory, or whether, in disregard of the Hague Conventions the occupant eliminates even the last traces of that effectiveness, the continuity of the occupied State is safeguarded, not by an act of will of the occupying power, but by a clear objective rule of international law. (7)

Not only was the continued occupation of Hawai'i by the United States a violation of international law, but of U.S. Constitutional law as well. To the point, a scholar of U.S. Constitutional law, Westel Willoughby, wrote in 1929:

> The constitutionality of the annexation of Hawai'i, by a simple legislative act, was strenuously contested at the time both in Congress and by the press. The right to annex by treaty was not denied (assuming the legitimacy of both parties—author), but it was denied that this might be done by a simple legislative act. Only by means of treaties, it was asserted, can the relations between States be governed, for a legislative act is necessarily without extraterritorial force—confined in its operation to the territory of the State by whose legislature it is enacted. (8)

The U.S., however, went even further, **declaring as void all bi-lateral treaties previously entered into between the nation of Hawai'i and other independent countries**, boldly and without regard for international law asserting:

> The existing treaties with the Hawaiian Islands with foreign nations shall forthwith cease and determine,

> being replaced by such treaties as may exist, or as may be hereafter concluded, between the United States and such foreign nations. (9)

To use the hypothetical analogy cited early in this book, suppose that the U.S., after having annexed Denmark against the will of the overwhelming majority of the Danes, had unilaterally declared that any treaties made between Denmark and England, France, Sweden, Norway, Germany, etc. were void by the stroke of a pen! On the contrary, a careful legal analysis will show that the Hawaiian Kingdom, as the legal sovereign entity, having dominion over the Hawaiian Islands, has been in suspended animation since January 17, 1893. International law also provides for the requirement that any occupying force utilize the laws of the country being occupied for the time being occupied (as for example, the U.S. post-war occupation of Japan), not the laws of the occupier itself. (10)

On the contrary, the U.S. government set up a system that amounted to a puppet government, with a governor appointed by the United States' president, not elected by the people. This system remained in placed until the purported "statehood" in 1959. Adding further insult to injury, as perceived by Hawaiians, was the wholesale unwanted alteration of citizenship. Instead of being citizens of Hawai'i, residents of Hawai'i were instantly designated citizens of the United States, and subject to a whole array of unfamiliar laws. The puppet nature of Hawaiian government remains today, as the "state" is subject to U.S. federal laws.

One of the clearest statements on the matter of sovereignty under duress from an occupying power occurs in the *British Manual of Military Law,* 1929:

> . . .the sovereignty of the legitimate owner of the territory is only temporarily latent, but it still exists and in no way passes to the occupant. The latter's rights are

> merely transitory, and he should only exercise such power as is necessary for the purpose of the war, the maintenance of order and safety, and the proper administration of the country. . .The occupant, therefore, must not treat the country as part of his own territory, nor consider the inhabitants as his lawful subjects. (11)

More to the point, according to the United States Basic Field Manual, Rules of Land Warfare,

> Military occupation is a question of fact. . .It does not transfer sovereignty to the occupant. ..the sovereignty of the occupied territory is not vested in the occupying power. The occupation is essentially provisional. (12)

It seems clear to this writer that a coerced transfer of power in 1893, unwanted by the overwhelming majority of people living in Hawai'i, together with an unwanted and, in fact, strenuously resisted "annexation" fraudulently obtained by military presence and by manipulation of imposters, leads to the inescapable conclusion that this **is** indeed a matter of occupation, extended for well over one hundred years, notwithstanding the further fraud of "statehood" which itself was based upon the two prior fraudulent actions. Most interestingly, when the United States has been pressed on this point, it cannot justify its actions, but essentially resorts to tacit "squatter's rights," saying in effect, "We are here and we aren't going." In legal terms, it is not necessary for Hawai'i to prove its continued sovereignty; *it is up to the United States to prove otherwise before an international body.*

> As the Hawaiian Kingdom's existence is a matter defined by international law, any challenge of its sovereignty must be made before an international tribunal possessing the proper jurisdiction to render such chal-

lenge unwarranted. To date, there has been no legal challenge by any other State or international organization to the continued existence of the legal personality of the Hawaiian Kingdom as an independent State in accordance with customary and conventional international law. Along these lines, Professor Marek asserts that the laws of occupation,

'. . .positively outlawed the creation of puppets as a means of indirectly violating the international occupation regime. It has branded them as illegal. Whatever their claims, they are unable to break the continuity of the occupied State to which they are in no way related, whether they take the form of puppet States or puppet governments. In the event of the creation by the occupant of a puppet State or States on the territory of the occupied State, the latter survives, with its legal status unchanged.' (13)

Chapter 8

Hawaiian Renaissance

It is generally agreed that the period of reawakening among Hawaiian people, and by cultural and political osmosis, the people of other nationalities in Hawai'i as well, began in 1970 with the Kalama Valley land struggle, the first of a series of efforts to beat back large profit-making developments of land for up-scale residents at the expense of those on the lower end of the scale. This author has some personal knowledge of this event, having been a direct supporter. It began with the announcement that all the people living on the land there, including some active farmers, would be evicted to make way for the development. Most left grudgingly, but a few hung on and were supported by some from the student movement that had formed to combat the war against Vietnam and to promote civil rights.

The land was owned by the Estate of Bernice Pauahi Bishop, the largest private landholder in Hawai'i with multi-billion dollar assets and enormous political clout. This power began with the accumulation of land by Ms. Bishop, a Hawaiian of the elite class, and her Caucasian banker husband, during the 1800s. When she died in the 1880s, her estate was put in trust for the benefit of the education of Hawaiian children. Thus began one of the two wealthiest school systems in Hawai'i which continues to prosper today: The Kamehameha Schools.

The anti-war and civil rights movement had been initiated by young people around the University of Hawai'i and supplemented by some from community colleges and high schools. The majority had been Caucasian in the beginning, but soon attracted those commonly and proudly called "local." Briefly, "local" means raised in Hawai'i, with overtones of being non-white. Thus, there is a separate category for Caucasians raised in Hawai'i—"local *haole.*" *Haole* (pronounced HOW lee) is often a derogatory term, especially for newcomers who really haven't a clue about what Hawaiian culture is all about. However, it can also be used simply as a description for white people. It all depends on the context. Being a "local *haole"* is definitely a step up in the social hierarchy, being a Caucasian person who has been around local people growing up and thus cognizant of the various nuances and mannerisms of local people.

During the Kalama Valley event, the young local activists, many of whom were Native Hawaiian, decided to assert their independence from the predominantly *haole* student movement. Though we *haoles* were willing if not eager to participate, while leaving strategic considerations to the local activists, we were asked (reasonably politely) to leave in order to allow for self-determination which was very important for the emerging Hawaiian base for this movement. The thrust of the movement at Kalama was to say "No!" to Bishop Estate, "you will not ruthlessly kick people off the land they have been working just so you can make big profits."

The symbolic head of the resistance to development was an elderly resolute pig farmer named George Santos, and people camped out around his property in defiance. Of course, Bishop Estate, with their power and "landlord rights" was able to muster the political and police force to squash the protest. His pigs were moved, as were the people resisting, and development proceeded. Today the valley is covered with well-manicured lawns fronting curbed sidewalks and homes built for upper middle class and beyond. But this was the beginning of numerous similar events all through the 1970s.

The first of two of the most successful of these land struggles, supported by a wide range of ethnicities and by now three generations of residents, was the Waiahole-

Waikane Valley resistance to yet another development scheme which would have displaced successful family farms in some of the best quality farm land in Hawai'i, blessed with rich soil and abundant rainfall. Many of the activists from the Kalama Valley struggle had deepened their political and economic education in the meantime and were able to unite with the farming community to resist, which they did in particular in two dramatic fashions—publicly burning the eviction notices and closing down the main highway with bodies and automobiles to force a resolution favorable to the people. The then-governor, George Ariyoshi, stepped in and arranged for the State (sic) of Hawai'i to purchase the large tract of land with the promise, later negotiated successfully, to provide long term leases to the farmers and divert development elsewhere.

The second major successful struggle for control of land was the island of Kaho'olawe, which, like Vieques in Puerto Rico, had been used since WW II as a bombing target, much to the dismay of Hawaiians who have always had a strong kinship with the land. During the 1970s, a few brave Hawaiians, mostly from the islands nearest—Maui and Moloka'i—would make excursions to the island, which was off-limits according to the U.S. Navy. Once there, their allies back on the main islands would notify the media and civil authorities that there were people on the island in order to forestall bombing raids. In due time, the "trespassers" would be captured, arrested, and removed. Tragically, during one of these cat-and-mouse events, two young men, George Helm, an accomplished musician as well as activist, and his friend, Kimo Mitchell, disappeared, never to be seen again.

After a number of these excursions, the matter of return of the island to the control of Hawai'i and cessation of bombing raids increasingly won the support not only of the overwhelming majority of Hawaiians, but by an independent poll, at least half of the general public across *ethnic lines*. This circumstance led the Republican Party to announce through

George Bush Sr. and the Hawai'i Republican candidate for U.S. Senate, Patricia Saiki, the permanent cessation of bombing and return of the island to "State" control, along with some measure of cleanup of old and unexploded bombs. While the move was greatly welcomed, Ms. Saiki still lost the race.

Fast forwarding to 2004 regarding military control of Hawaiian land, according to an American Friends Service Committee (AFSC) Hawai'i report, which cites several official sources including "Department of Defense Base Structure Report, Fiscal Year 2003 Baseline," the following table reveals the areas by major islands, plus one minor island:

O'ahu	84,797 acres out of 382,148 acres, or 22.2%
Hawai'i	109,903 acres out of 2,578,073 acres, or 4.3%
Kaua'i	4,498 acres out of 353,484 acres, or 1.3%
Moloka'i	374 acres out of 166,425 acres, or 0.2%
Maui	15 acres out of 465,472 acres, or 0.003%
Kaula	108 acres out of 158 acres, or 68.3% (1)

It should be noted that this is what is under military control, which includes "ownership" along with long term leases, from either private or "state" ownership, and that this amount of land is what is left AFTER the return of the **entire island** of Kaho'olawe, which is about 45 square miles or 28,880 acres, as mentioned, due to inexorable pressure from the people of Hawai'i. The most striking feature is that of military control over **22% of the most populated island by far** (2) at 567 people per square kilometer, compared to 72.8 people per square kilometer for all the islands combined. (3.) It is also important to note that a significant portion of the remaining 78% of the land area of O'ahu consists of steep mountains that are uninhabitable, but which are of great value for water retention and for esthetic reasons.

The AFSC report also cites "828 Military Contamination sites in Hawai'i and 70 Military Munitions Response Program sites (Note: This does not include the active military ranges or special munitions clean up projects, e.g., Kaho'olawe, Makua, Waikane, Schofield, Pohakuloa, Kaula)"(4)

In terms of population, 53,658 active duty personnel are stationed on O'ahu, with 54,036 overall.(5) If one includes dependents, the figure rises to 83,329, or 6.9% of the population of Hawai'i. (6) If one includes retired military, the figure rises to 112,000 or 16.1%. (7)

Returning to the broad picture, besides these vigorous land struggles, from around 1970 onward there has been a powerful resurgence in Hawaiian culture, manifested in highly popular Hawaiian language classes at high school and college level, and immersion projects in which children are taught every subject in the Hawaiian language, and for the first time in several generations, there exist young people fluent in Hawaiian, outside the small, sparsely populated island of Ni'ihau, where Hawaiian is the principal language.

Music, in the form of countless songs in the Hawaiian language, and hula troupes (called *halau*) are both flourishing. Besides the graceful slow hula movements (*auana* style) with which Westerners are familiar, the ancient hula called *kahiko* style in which both men and women participate has been revived. Perhaps one way to describe it to those who have not seen it is to think of it as a fusion of dance and martial arts, like karate or kung fu.

Yet another exciting manifestation of Hawaiian culture is the reintroduction of the long voyages of double-hulled canoes. By long, we are not talking about those between the Hawaiian Islands, but between Hawai'i and Tahiti, New Zealand, finally Rapa Nui, otherwise known as Easter Island. These trips can be thousands of miles. Most importantly, they have been accomplished without the use of any modern instruments, but by broad knowledge of the celestial sky and keen observation of ocean currents, cloud formations, bird populations, etc.

These voyages have rekindled an immense pride throughout the Polynesian societies as people have come to understand that these types of conscious and deliberate voyages were being made by their ancestors over one thousand years before Columbus made his historic voyage to North America. Without doubt, they were the best navigators and sailors in the world at the time. People interested in learning more can consult the Polynesian Voyaging Society.

All of these activities prepared the ground for a deepened study of history and the conclusion that not only was the imposition of U.S. law upon Hawai'i unjust, it was blatantly illegal under both U.S. Constitutional law and international law, as previously discussed. The most dramatic mass event occurred on January 17, 1993, the exact 100th anniversary of the overthrow of the Queen. Some 12,000 people assembled, mostly Hawaiian, but with welcomed support from non-Hawaiians. This writer was part of a small delegation of Hawai'i Green Party members who pledged support for sovereignty in a broad sense, yet to be defined at the time.

Two years later came the discovery in the Library of Congress by Hawaiian activist Noenoe Silva of the "Monster Petition" (so-named because of the tens of thousands of names listed). The sight of the names of ancestors protesting impending annexation in 1897 kindled great pride and determination among people of Hawaiian ancestry. The many pages of names were posted on large sheets covering hundreds of square feet of wall space at the Bishop Museum, a central location in Honolulu for research on Hawai'i and other Pacific Island peoples. For non-Hawaiians like this author, it was likewise an inspiration, not because of any family connection, but from the understanding of the innate drive of people to resist injustice then, and that struggle's connection to the present.

As a result of this upsurge of protest and assertion of right to self-determination, the U.S. government, in collaboration with the U.S. Congressional delegation from Hawai'i, offered a rare public apology during the early stages of the

Clinton Administration, on Nov. 23, 1993—100 years plus a few months after the overthrow of the Queen. This Apology Resolution reads, in part:

> Whereas, prior to the arrival of the first Europeans in 1778, the Native Hawaiian people lived in a highly organized, self-sufficient, subsistent social system based on communal land tenure with a sophisticated language, culture, and religion; . . .
>
> Whereas, from 1826 until 1893, the United States recognized the independence of the Kingdom of Hawaii, extended full and complete diplomatic recognition to the Hawaiian Government, and entered into treaties and conventions with the Hawaiian Monarchs to govern commerce and navigation in 1826, 1842, 1849, 1875 and 1887: . .
>
> Whereas, on January 14, 1893, John L. Stevens (hereafter referred to in this resolution as the "United States Minister"), the United States Minister assigned to the sovereign and independent Kingdom of Hawaii conspired with a small group of non-Hawaiian residents of the Kingdom of Hawaii, including citizens of the United States, to overthrow the indigenous and lawful Government of Hawaii;
>
> Whereas, in pursuance of the conspiracy to overthrow the Government of Hawaii, the United States Minister and the naval representatives of the United States caused armed naval forces of the United States to invade the sovereign Hawaiian nation on January 16, 1893, and to position themselves near the Hawaiian Government buildings and the Iolani Palace to intimidate Queen Liliuokalani and her Government;

Whereas, on the afternoon of January 17, 1893, a Committee of Safety that represented the American and European sugar planters, descendants of missionaries, and financiers deposed the Hawaiian monarchy and proclaimed the establishment of a Provisional Government;

Whereas, the United States Minister thereupon extended diplomatic recognition to the Provisional Government that was formed by the conspirators without the consent of the Native Hawaiian people or the lawful Government of Hawaii and in violation of treaties between the two nations and of international law; . . .

Whereas, in a message to Congress on December 18, 1893, President Grover Cleveland reported fully and accurately on the illegal acts of the conspirators, described such acts as an "act of war, committed with the participation of a diplomatic representative of the United States and without authority of Congress," and acknowledged that by such acts the government of a peaceful and friendly people was overthrown;

Whereas, President Cleveland further concluded that a 'substantial wrong has thus been done which a due regard for our national character as well as the rights of the injured people requires we should endeavor to repair' and called for the restoration of the Hawaiian monarchy; . . .

Whereas, although the Provisional Government was able to obscure the role of the United States in the illegal overthrow of the Hawaiian monarchy, it was unable to rally the support from two-thirds of the Senate to ratify a treaty of annexation;. . . .

Whereas, on July 7, 1898, as a consequence of the Spanish-American War, President McKinley signed the Newlands Joint Resolution that provided for the annexation of Hawaii; . . .

Whereas, the indigenous Hawaiian people never directly relinquished their claims to their inherent sovereignty as a people or over their national lands to the United States, either through their monarchy or through a plebiscite or referendum; ....

Now, therefore, be it
Resolved by the Senate and House of Representatives of the United States of America in Congress assembled,

SECTION 1. ACKNOWLEDGMENT AND APOLOGY.
The Congress-

(1)on the occasion of the 100th anniversary of the illegal overthrow of the Kingdom of Hawaii on January 17, 1893, acknowledges the historical significance of this event which resulted in the suppression of the inherent sovereignty of the Native Hawaiian people;

(2) recognizes and commends the efforts of reconciliation initiated by the State of Hawaii and the United Church of Christ with Native Hawaiians;

(3) apologizes to Native Hawaiians on behalf of the people of the United States for the overthrow of the Kingdom of Hawaii on January 17, 1893 with the participation of agents and citizens of the United States, and the deprivation of the rights of Native Hawaiians to self-determination;

(4) expresses its commitment to acknowledge the ramifications of the overthrow of the Kingdom of Hawaii, in order to provide a proper foundation for reconciliation between the United States and the Native Hawaiian people; and

(5) urges the President of the United States to also acknowledge the ramifications of the overthrow of the Kingdom of Hawaii and to support reconciliation efforts between the United States and the Native Hawaiian people. (8)

Fair-minded people will certainly regard this statement as a major step in the right direction. An acknowledgment and apology has been made by the government responsible for the burglary of an entire nation. But what about restitution? Can the theft of hundreds of billions (in current value) of property, and the incalculable value of self-determination be ignored and swept under the rug as nonessential? Of course not! When a thief is caught with the goods in hand, in addition to prosecution, he/she must return the stolen goods! That is elementary. Apparently the U.S. government wants to "let bygones be bygones." Not so fast, Uncle Sam! The apology is just phase one of a necessary process of *ho'oponopono,* the Hawaiian word for "making matters right," in the sense of "just," "honorable," "morally correct." The result must be regained national sovereignty.

Furthermore, this apology misses the point. It treats the matter as if the offense was solely to the people of Hawaiian ancestry *as an indigenous ethnic group,* rather than to all subjects of Hawai'i, no matter what ethnicity. It is not a matter of relative self-determination of the Hawaiian ethnic group within the context of a state of the United States, but in fact the **much larger issue** of ending the 100+ year occupation of a foreign (to the United States) nation. (9)

Yet another contemporary manifestation of this effort to be free of U.S. military domination came in 2004 as people on the Big Island (Hawai'i), as well as other islands, organized to resist yet another military encroachment: an attempt by the U.S. to base a Stryker Brigade there, over the strenuous objections of residents who see many problems. The Stryker is a mammoth 19-ton tank-like heavily armored machine whose presence would be anything but benign. From incessant noise to massive dust pollution to destruction of fragile plant and animal life as well as being just the latest of a long chain of military intrusions, this encroachment is not wanted. In June of 2004, public testimony was held in Hilo, Hawaii, after previous highly contested hearings on Oahu, on the matter of the proposed U.S. Army Stryker Brigade. The military and political powers in Washington propose a plan to acquire yet another 109,000 acres of precious land in Hawai'i for military use, specifically for training with Strykers over some culturally and environmentally sensitive areas. Some 70 people turned out to testify, along with numerous other spectators. Of these, only three supported the plan during the first half of the period allotted, with 28 speaking against. (10)

Here are some of the host of issues raised in objection (in summary form) during that testimony. Not only can dust be a nuisance, but for people with allergies, it can make the air quality miserable and be a health hazard. Furthermore, tourists of substantial means come to Hawai'i for its peaceful serenity, a quality environment, and aloha spirit. The last thing they want is to be confronted with 19-ton behemoths charging around, even at a distance. It would be easy to foresee that the local economy could be terribly impacted by irate tourists who have spent their money and found such an intrusion. As the word spread to the U.S. and other countries, and the numbers reduced, as happened during the Gulf War, workers would be laid off and niche businesses that rely on the tourist trade would suffer. (11)

Some of the most powerful and important telescopes in the world are located on the Big Island of Hawai'i because of its remote location (away from most smog and dust pollution), amiable climate, and nearly 14,000 foot mountain peaks of Mauna Kea and Mauna Loa. It takes no imagination to see how this important scientific research could be jeopardized by both dust and vibrations from exploding ordnance. Part of the plan calls for 23,000 acres of land on the slopes of Mauna Kea. But even the peaceful presence of an ever-growing number of huge telescopes, without taking into account Hawaiian sensibilities for use of the land, has become a sore point for Hawaiians. Even aloha has its limits!

Still on the threat to science, and to Hawaiian culture, it is claimed that there are some 250 archeological sites within the huge Pohakuloa Training Area, the site planned for the Stryker Brigade. The more it is militarized, the more the threat to such sites. (12)

In the past decade, U.S. military forces have been using depleted uranium (DU) in battlefield situations, which means they must have previously tested it. Where? (13) The advantage of DU is that it is substantially heavier than lead, and so when projected, has more mass with which to penetrate its target, especially opposing tanks. However, on impact, it shatters into fine dust particles. As a solid, it is not particularly dangerous, but as dust it is inhaled and can be devastating on the human body. It is suspected that large numbers of American forces, not to mention countless numbers of Iraqis, have been fatally infected with depleted uranium from both the first Bush Gulf War and the second Bush Gulf War. Is Hawai'i subject to this lethal material? Will U.S. military personnel be training with it in the arid Pohakuloa region, contaminating hundreds of generations of people? By what authority can such atrocious behavior against a peace-loving people be justified? Even with the present level of toxic contamination at military sites, at present rates of cleanup, it will take centuries to complete. Such a massive intrusion to Hawaiian life even threatens undisturbed use of such facilities as a Girl Scout Camp and Mauna Kea "State" Park. (14) Threats of forced evacuation hover like "vog," the unique combination of fog and volcanic ash produced from the continually erupting Kilauea crater.

Finally, with regard to the cultural-political level, military authorities even attempted on some occasions to deny peaceful legal protest by insisting that signs not be permitted, a violation of the Constitutionally guaranteed right to peacefully assemble and request a redress of grievances. Collectively, continued military presence generates fear, intimidation, and even hopelessness against so powerful a foe. People had the sense of the whole affair of "more land to U.S. military and disregard for Hawaiian sensitivities" was already a "done deal" in Washington with the collusion of some or all of the Congressional delegation from Hawai'i. Such decisions, or course, fly in the face of the ancient respect for nature and the precious spirit of aloha, which remains real and a vital aspect of Hawaiian life despite being assaulted by military occupation and intrusion and by super commercialization by international corporate interests.

One response of the United States to this resistance of U.S. domination has been to try to coopt the movement by offering some relief through the Akaka Bill, named for Hawai'i's junior (though still very senior) Sen. Daniel Akaka, a Native Hawaiian, since retired January 2013, together with his colleague the late Sen. Daniel Inouye. This bill, which has been languishing in Congress for years, attempts to give to Native Hawaiians a status similar to that "enjoyed" by Native Americans, that is to say, a certain amount of autonomy and perhaps some financial compensation, but all the while under the watchful eyes of the federal government which would hold ultimate authority.

But even this is too much for the far right wing who denounce it as creating a separate "privileged" class of people in Hawai'i, with the same point of view as those who have opposed affirmative action as unjustified, on the grounds that everyone ought to have the same starting point. This position is, of course, fundamentally racist in that it obscures and negates the initial virulent racism of past **and** present generations of rulers that has practiced severe discrimination, slavery, lynchings, theft of land and assets, to outright genocide against native peoples. No way has the starting line toward "pursuit of happiness" been the same. Affirmative action has simply been a rather feeble but important initiative to reverse at least a small portion of the disadvantage caused by such practices.

On its face, the Akaka Bill is an attempt to apply the concept of affirmative action to Hawaiians. But its underlying, and more sinister, objective is to undermine the sovereignty movement's attempt to achieve real independence by keeping the movement *contained* within the framework of U.S. jurisdiction. Many Hawaiians see through this ploy, however, and oppose the bill vigorously from the left. The central issue to know is that the Akaka Bill, by virtue of being a piece of *U.S. domestic law legislation,* in no way affects the legitimate assertions of the right to re-establish the Hawaiian Kingdom as an independent nation. One clear voice in this matter was raised by a Hawaiian woman journalist, Keala Kelly, at a forum on the Bill in 2005. Here are some excerpts from her speech:

> This legislation is primarily about money—it's about using American laws to control the land and resources of Hawai'i and the political and cultural destiny of Kanaka Maoli who are the rightful heirs to the 1.8 million acres of Crown and Government lands. We are told that it will protect 70 million federal dollars per year and millions of dollars in trust assets, but there's no guarantee for any of that in the bill—and truth is that if we controlled our own land and collected rent and taxes on that land we wouldn't need any federal money

and would be well on our way to self determination. . . During the past 4 years I've had the privilege of listening to, interviewing or filming Hawaiians from all over who oppose this legislation. There are 3 things they have in common:

(1)Many Hawaiians see federal recognition as a threat to their legal options for true self-determination under international law—and see this bill as a way of exchanging those rights for the American version, which means the plenary powers of congress—and that means no power for Hawaiians at all;

(2)They see it as an attempt by the United States to pressure us into signing over title to the Crown and Government Lands of the Hawaiian Kingdom;

And (3)—they believe it is an insult to the legacy of our ali'i and that it undermines our spiritual and cultural kuleana (authority, jurisdiction—author) as Hawaiians. Despite the assertion by others who insist that Hawaiians are no different than any average U.S. citizen—Hawaiians who know their history often see themselves as Hawaiian citizens, not Americans. They know the Organic Act of 1900 did not make them American citizens, it made citizens of the phony Republic of Hawai'i into Americans. Kanaka Maoli were not citizens of the Republic. The Kanaka Maoli never acquiesced to either the Fake Republic of Hawai'i or to the United States. Hawaiians are called citizens of the U.S. but that has been done without consent. . . .

If we look at America through the eyes of our kupuna (grandparents, ancestors—author), what we see is the same country that helped overthrow the Kingdom. We see the same country whose political, economic and

> legal system has displaced the Kanaka Maoli and used our homeland as a playground and a military outpost while developing what is now the largest arsenal in the world. . . .
>
> This bill places our assets in the Dept. of Interior, an agency that is presently defrauding our indigenous friends on the continent of billions of dollars worth of their trust assets and is refusing to comply with orders from its own government's federal courts. Imagine what they can do to us with all the practice they've had on the Indians. We can't even get the state of Hawai'i to inventory our lands, do we really think we're going to get anywhere with the feds? And this legislation was created by the feds. It emerged from the offices of Senator Inouye and Senator Akaka. . . .
>
> Hawaiians oppose this bill because they know it's an attempt to make us acquiesce to the overthrow. Hawaiians know that if the state and federal government manipulates us into surrendering title to the C & G lands, those lands will be opened to further militarization.
>
> We know that if we continue to allow the practice of war on our 'aina, if we allow bombs and poisons to be planted in our 'aina, then it will follow that we as a people shall reap what we sow. Right now the largest crop and subsequent export of Hawai'i is murder and suffering via the U.S. military industrial complex—not food, and certainly no aloha. (15)

Through a convoluted but rational manner, the legal construct for reinstituting the Hawaiian monarchy has been proposed via the Hawaiian Kingdom Trust Company, which then appointed an *Acting* Regent, in the absence of any surviving members of the government of 1893. The mechanisms employed are beyond the scope of this work, but it is this *Acting* Regent, along with other appointed officers, who presented the case for an independent Hawai'i, to the International Court of Arbitration at The Hague in December of 2000.

This case did not *directly* challenge the United States, which refused an offer to be a party to the arbitration, but dealt with the potential liability of the newly reinstituted Hawaiian Government to protect its subjects, and in particular, one Hawaiian man named Lance Larsen, who attempted to follow Hawaiian Kingdom law, but in the process violated "state" and county ordinances, for which he had been jailed. He sought to ascertain the relation between himself as a subject of the Hawaiian Monarchy, and that government, which, due to U.S. intervention and occupation, has been rendered powerless for over one hundred years. (16)

> The *Acting* Council (Council of Regency—author) serves as the *de facto* organ of the Hawaiian Kingdom State. It does not represent any particular group of individuals organized by ethnic origin or by common ideology. The *Acting* Council is limited and operates within the framework of Hawaiian domestic law, which is defined by the 1864 Constitution and the statutes lawfully enacted by the legislative assembly previous to the illegal constitution of 1887 and subsequent occupation of the country by the United States. (17)

The International Court took the matter seriously, and gave the Hawaiian delegation the utmost respect, even to the point of flying the Hawaiian flag at the site during the hearing. The net result, after the information cited in this book was presented there, amounted to an acknowledgment that the matter could not be resolved without the participation of the other affected party, the United States. The conclusions reached by the prestigious tribunal were presented on Feb. 5, 2001, including the following statements:

"A perusal of the material discloses that in the nineteenth century the Hawaiian Kingdom existed as an independent State recognized as such by the United States of America, the United Kingdom and various other States, including by exchanges of diplomatic or consular representatives and the conclusion of treaties." (18)

> Further: that the tribunal '. . .cannot rule on the lawfulness of the conduct of the respondent (Hawaiian Government) in the present case if the decision would entail or require, as a necessary foundation for the decision between the parties, an evaluation of the lawfulness of the conduct of the United States of America, or, indeed, the conduct of any other State which is not a party to the proceedings before the Tribunal.' (19)

Nevertheless, the Tribunal submitted as an attachment to its conclusions, the entire *Message of U.S. President Grover Cleveland on December 18, 1893 AND the 1993 Joint Resolution Apologizing for the illegal overthrow of the Hawaiian Kingdom.* (20) These two vital documents are included as appendices A and B herein. Further commentary has appeared in international law journals, such as the following two excerpts:

> Because international tribunals lack the power of joinder that national courts enjoy, it is possible—as a result of procedural maneuvering alone—for legitimate international legal disputes to escape just adjudication. For example, in Larsen, the United States commanded an enviable litigation posture: Even though the United States admitted its illegal overthrow of the Hawaiian Kingdom, it repeatedly refused to consent to international arbitration. (21)

> The law of occupation as defined in the 1907 Hague Convention protects the international personality of the occupied state, even in the absence of effectiveness. Furthermore, the legal order of the occupied State (Hawaiian Kingdom) remains intact, although its effectiveness is greatly diminished by the fact of occupation. (22)

Despite the absence of legal justifications on the part of the United States regarding its extended occupation of Hawai'i, the situation remains one of "How do you get the elephant out of the house if he doesn't want to go?"

Photograph credit: Ed Greevy/Mutual Publishing Honolulu.

An estimated 12,000 people rallied on January 17, 1993, exactly 100 years after the U.S.-assisted sabotage of the legitimate government of Hawai'i.

Photograph credit: Ed Greevy/Mutual Publishing Honolulu.

Chapter 9

Parallel Paradigm—Liberating Lithuania

To address the question often raised that the matter of independent nationhood for Hawai'i has long been settled, and that proponents of sovereignty should just "forget it," I shall introduce the important case of Lithuania, a small country in Western Europe just north of Poland bordering the Baltic Sea. Long dominated by Poland and Germany, and invaded periodically by Russians, and subsequently the Soviet Union, Lithuanian independent status seemed to many to be a hopeless dream with negligible chance of coming to fruition. I will review here the evolution of the realities faced by proponents of Lithuanian independence and their eventual success.

While it may seem to some that this is an unnecessary digression, in some regards, this is the **most** important chapter, for, by way of **vital recent historical example, it points the way to victory**, by overcoming the defeatist viewpoint, so often heard, "Well, it would be nice to achieve sovereignty, but the U.S. will never let us have it." The parallels of Lithuanian history to that of Hawai'i with regard to sovereignty are striking. This is a *clear historical example* of how a nation with remarkably similar circumstances *achieved its freedom from an imperial power.* This example, among others that could be cited, negates the pessimistic view that Hawai'i's status is permanently fixed. The analogy comes to mind of a "fixed" tomcat. Important lessons on the conduct of peaceful resistance can be learned in this courageous and prolonged struggle for liberation.

At the outbreak of World War I, Lithuania was sandwiched between two huge powers, Russia and Germany, with Poland as a buffer on the German side. At the time, they were dominated by Russia, which demanded the use of Russian language as a way to minimize Lithuanian identity, a standard practice of any occupying imperial power. (The same policy prevailed in Hawai'i with regard to the use of English, as we have noted.) However, with the incursion of German forces that drove the Russians back, German became the required language. Even letters written to one another in Lithuanian were declared illegal. Further, the occupying Germans seized food and other daily goods for their own use with little regard for the needs of the population of Lithuania. Freedom of movement was restricted. Infractions of rules could be severely punished. (1)

However, despite repressive conditions, Lithuanian patriots did not give up, but organized clandestinely. Their compatriots in the United States, free from immediate repression connected with the warring parties, raised their voices, holding meetings in Chicago and New York in 1914 demanding that the right of self determination be recognized internationally. (2)

Lithuanian patriots shrewdly used excellent timing to proclaim this independence—at the conclusion of the war in 1918 when all their neighbors were exhausted from the effort. Further history in their favor was the successful Marxist-Leninist revolution in Russia and its desperate need to consolidate power, feed a starving population, and combat incursions from other powers scared witless over the prospect of Bolshevism. (3)

With Germany still trying to retain influence and the Russians on guard against foreign aggression, the newly won independence was shaky. Gradually the Germans withdrew their army and on July 12, 1920 the Lithuanian-Russian peace treaty was signed in which it was stated ". . .without any Reservations, Russia recognizes Lithuania's independence and self-government with all its due jurisdictional rights, and with good will renounces for all times, all rights of Russian sovereignty which she had over the Lithuanian nation and its territories." (4) This statement is of significance in that **it unequivocally renounces claims to Lithuania,** a promise to be shattered a mere twenty years later. These two approaches to integrity in foreign relations illustrate one of many differences between leadership by Lenin and by Stalin, the former upholding the right of nations to self-determination as a principle, and the latter only as expedient, or not, as he chose.

The Lithuanian Constituent Assembly met on May 15, 1920 and ratified their Declaration of Independence with these words: "The Constituent Assembly of Lithuania expressing the will of the people of Lithuania, proclaims the restored independent Lithuanian state, as a democratic republic, with ethnographic boundaries and free of any state ties which had previously bound it with other states." (5) Among the provisions enacted were measures on land reform and full rights of citizenship regardless of sex, nationality, or religion. (6)

Peace and independence was short-lived. With the rise to power of the Nazi Party, tensions heightened all over Europe. On Sept. 1, 1939, Germany invaded Poland, and shortly afterward forces of the U.S.S.R. occupied portions of eastern Poland. Lithuania declared neutrality, but graciously gave refuge to fleeing Polish people and treated them humanely. (7) An aggressive German policy cared little for the neutrality of Lithuania. An incident occurred that bears a stirring resemblance to the coerced conditional surrender of Queen Lili'uokalani. After issuing a bellicose statement, ships were dispatched. ". . .six hours before the signing of the treaty the German battleship *Deutschland* steamed out of Swinemuende with Hitler and his escort, en route to Klaipeda. (a Lithuanian city—author) The armada sailing with the *Deutschland* included the battleship *Graf Spee*, the cruisers *Nuremberg, Leipzig*, and *Koeln*, as well as a number of destroyers, torpedo boats, and lesser craft." (8) The message was unmistakable: sign an unfavorable treaty granting acceptance of unwanted German presence or invite a worse fate. They signed.

> Clandestine newspapers representing all parties were printed in specially constructed cellars well hidden from the prying eyes of the Gestapo. It was no easy task to organize their publication and to provide them with paper, which, of course, could not be obtained in the free market, when the entire country was covered with a network of German spies. Well trained assistants were needed; a system of counterespionage against the Gestapo had to be organized; and data provided compromising the Nazis. Moreover, after printing, the distribution of these newspapers was both difficult and dangerous. . . .Even humorous and satirical periodicals were printed and widely circulated, and special publications warned the people against German agents, spies, and traitors. . . . The total issue of all secret newspapers would be almost equal to that of the so-called legal press. Considering that every copy of a secret paper passed from hand to hand, it is safe to assume that the clandestine press reached most of the inhabitants of the country. (9)

With the outbreak of WW II commencing with the German invasion of neighboring Poland and German-U.S.S.R. non-aggression pact, pressure was put on Lithuanians by the U.S.S.R. to allow Soviet troops to be stationed in their country. The alternatives seemed to be either allow this concession or risk invasion. So, only seven months after being coerced into an unfavorable treaty with Germany, Lithuania signed away partial sovereignty to the U.S.S.R.

This treaty, signed on Oct. 10, 1939, allowed for "a strictly limited number of Soviet ground troops and air forces." The seventh article of the treaty specified: "The execution of this treaty in no way should be an interference in the internal affairs of the contracting parties, especially in the economic and social system by military means, and generally means the principle of noninterference in internal matters . . .Yet six months later, the Soviets violated all of the treaties concluded by the two states and used force against Lithuania and against the neighboring states. . ." (10)

During the morning of June 15, 1940, the Soviet government issued demonstrably false accusations against Lithuania as a pretext for occupation, giving only eight hours notice to respond to provocative demands. No agreement was reached within the Lithuanian government, and hours later the Soviet occupation of Lithuania began. (11) The occupation was to last fifty years, except for the brief setback during Nazi occupation.

As the intent of the Soviet Union became more evident, patriotic Lithuanians resigned or went into exile, to be replaced by compliant people who satisfied the occupier's desire for a facade of self government but were in essence puppets of the U.S.S.R. (Doesn't this sound just like the "Provisional Government" and "Republic of Hawai'i" with regard to the U.S.A?) Part of the methodology involved blatant fraud. (Where have we seen this before?) Documents were prepared and published, allegedly signed by many Lithuanians, some of whom had not given their assent, while others did so under duress. Similarly some Lithuanians discovered they were running for office when they read the newspapers published by the occupied forces, and threatened with reprisals when they tried to protest. The election featuring these so-called "candidates" was held only a week later! The "election" amounted to having the names read in a public meeting and "consent" granted by acclamation. To ensure desired results, the authorities arrested some 2000 civic and political leaders two days before the event. Furthermore, voting was mandatory, with the punishment being the designation as a "people's enemy." (12) This fraudulent "election" was then used subsequently to confer "legitimacy" to the puppet regime, just as voting eligibility rules in post-1893 Hawai'i by the *coup* plotters required prospective eligible voters to disavow support for the monarchy.

A review of these proceedings was made in the U.S. a decade later, in 1953. The United States House of Representatives' "Select Committee to Investigate the 'Incorporation' of the Baltic States into the U.S.S.R." declared

> . . .it is clear and proven beyond doubt that Estonia, Latvia, and Lithuania were taken over by force and illegally incorporated into the Soviet Union. Every Soviet assertion that the July, 1940 elections were free and voluntary or that the parliament assembled as a result of these 'elections' legitimately appealed for admission into the Soviet Union as a Soviet Republic is an unfounded lie. (13)

The fact that these times were at the height of cold war hysteria and the infamous McCarthy era whose zealots vilified the slightest hint of communism does not invalidate the reality of the situation. It is interesting to note, however, how utterly blind the government of the United States can be to its own parallel "unfounded lie" regarding the incorporation of Hawai'i in a manner nearly identical.

Shortly after the bogus "request" to join the U.S.S.R. was made, "the diplomatic representatives of Lithuania abroad presented their solemn protest against the falsification of the will of the Lithuanian people to the governments to which they were accredited, and unanimously condemned the Soviet aggression and the seizure of their state. A number of Western democratic states declined to recognize the incorporation and endorsed the continued activities of the Lithuanian diplomatic and consular representatives." (14)

In mid 1940, a series of measures were taken to exterminate religion, including destruction of religious books. Income to clergy was deleted and several priests were shot and others imprisoned on the grounds that beliefs can be coerced. (15) Furthermore, "The Russian language is foisted upon all the non-Russian nations, including Lithuania. Russification is advanced through the schools, theaters, and literature. The Russian language is introduced in the first year of primary school and is taught through all of the classes to the university level. . . .In some classes, children are placed with the children of the Russian colonists and forced to learn Russian. Russian songs are even taught in nursery schools." (16)

Substitute "American" for "Russian," and "Hawaiian" for "Lithuanian" and the same oppressive policies are evident. Such policies have continued for more than one hundred years in Hawai'i. Imagine the impact on consciousness over such a long span! Yet Native Hawaiians and their allies are in pursuit of justice and truth, are rediscovering the past, and are charting new ground on the voyage to liberation. A dramatic upsurge in interest in the study of Hawaiian language and music since the 1970s is only one indication of what is often called the Hawaiian Renaissance. Struggles over the use and control of land is another arena in this regard, along with a re-examination of history.

Despite many parallels between the experiences of Lithuania and Hawai'i there clearly are differences as well. There is, for example, no parallel to the forced deportations of thirty to forty thousand Lithuanians within a few days in 1941, often with as little as fifteen minutes to gather belongings and assemble all family members. (17) On the other hand, to my knowledge, there was nothing in Lithuania to parallel the more than a century of startling decline in native population from diseases and despair that occurred in Hawai'i prior to the overthrow of the Queen. Likewise, geographic and cultural differences are obvious as well. But on the key issue of national sovereignty, the parallels are striking.

No sooner had the U.S.S.R. begun these transformations than war broke out between the military titans of Europe with Germany's attack on the U.S.S.R. While the initial response from some Lithuanians was positive, due to daily oppression from the Soviet side, the Nazi regime had little use for Lithuanian assertion of independence. One brutal occupation was substituted for another. A description of Nazi atrocities is not required, as their treatment of non-Germans is well known. The tide of the war began to turn in the winter of 1943-44 and accelerated into 1944, with the Soviet army gradually reestablishing their occupation.

One of the principal means of conquest was the forced collectivization of farm land. Those who resisted were deported to the U.S.S.R., from where many did not return. The numbers ranged into the hundreds of thousands. "There are no exact figures on how many were deported. It is estimated that during the 1944-1951 period, about 350,000 persons were deported, which would comprise about twelve percent of the Lithuanian population. The unfortunates were sent to Soviet 'work camps' in the Soviet Union's far north or east, where the cruel climate, hard work, and meager rations caused the death of most of them." (18)

Meanwhile, large numbers of Russians migrated to Lithuania, which had relatively better conditions. The effect of this in-migration combined with forced outbound migration of some of the most capable and articulate Lithuanians had the inevitable effect of diluting effective resistance to the unwanted occupation. Although nominally, Lithuanians had important rights, in reality all significant decisions were made in Moscow. (19)

Prior to 1917, Lenin had forged an alliance between farmers and workers for the successful purpose of overthrowing the Czar and the successor government. He would have been shocked to see the coercion applied to these same classes of people in Lithuania by the very government he had founded only 30 years before. Lenin, unlike Stalin, had advocated voluntary cooperation and leading by example, not force, when dealing with these two classes of people.

During the unstable period when the Soviet occupation was under siege from the German advance at the beginning of the war, the Lithuanian underground achieved remarkable success, broadcasting news of liberation from the U.S.S.R., capturing large numbers of weapons, and freeing some 2000 political prisoners. Lithuanians who had been coerced into joining the Soviet army defected by the thousands and joined the resistance. (20)

After the end of WW II, resistance to Russian occupation had to take place mostly in the form of passive resistance such as boycotts of elections and Russian holidays, as well as the promotion of Lithuanian patriotic songs, even into primary schools. Courageous students produced flyers denouncing Soviet occupation and upholding Lithuanian independence. Workers and farmers resisted as they were able as well. (21)

Subsequent to the decisive failure to take Stalingrad, the Nazi command attempted to recruit Lithuanians to replace fallen soldiers, to no avail. While Lithuanians would fiercely fight invading forces, it would be on their terms and under Lithuanian control not German. When the Nazis ordered general mobilization into their army, Lithuanians responded with passive resistance by not showing up and by disappearing. Despite Nazi reprisals, Lithuanians were steadfast. (22)

At the height of Nazi repression, and with the recent history of Soviet occupation in mind, on Feb. 16, 1944, the Supreme Committee for Liberation of Lithuania (VLIK) issued a profound declaration, which reads in part:

> To the Lithuanian People!
> The Lithuanian nation, endeavoring to liberate Lithuania from the occupation and to restore the functioning of Lithuania's sovereign organs, temporarily

impeded by foreign forces, stands in need of a united political leadership. With this aim in view, the Lithuanian political groups, as exponents of the nation's political thought and as instruments of its application, have agreed to unite all forces for common action and have created the Supreme Committee for Liberation of Lithuania.

The Supreme Committee for Liberation of Lithuania entering upon its duties, declares that:

1. The freedom of the Lithuanian nation and the independence of the Lithuanian state are indispensable conditions for the nation's existence and well-being.
2. The sovereign State of Lithuania has not disappeared by reason of its occupation of the Soviet Union on the 15th of June, 1940, and the other diverse acts perpetrated by force and fraud under cover of that occupation resulting in disruption of the functions of the sovereign organs of the State, were brought to an end by the popular revolt of the Nation on June 23, 1941, and the functions of the sovereign organs of the State were temporarily resumed by the Provisional Government.
3. After the liberation of Lithuania from the occupation, the Constitution of 1938 will remain in force until it is appropriately amended in a legal manner. (23)

Further provisions cite the need to maintain truly democratic procedures, eliminate misunderstandings, raise an army, and maintain international contacts with Lithuanians abroad and with nations that recognize the rights of Lithuanians to re-establish self-determination. (24)

Meanwhile, the Soviet Union had achieved the upper hand versus Germany and considered Lithuanian part of Soviet territory. "After more than three years of Nazi occupation, the exhausted Lithuanian people looked forward to an Allied victory and the restoration of their independent state." (25)

During the period of 1944 to 1952, the number of Lithuanians killed during resistance or captured and executed is estimated at thirty to fifty thousand. Yet they persevered. The strategic thinking at the time was that Germany was near defeat and that subsequently the Western Allies would carry on the war by attacking the Soviet Union. Accordingly, the thinking went, it was necessary to mobilize the nation in anticipation of imminent liberation. (26)

Into 1945, the resistance had significant success against the second Soviet occupation and against the Lithuanian collaborators, using effective guerrilla methods, striking hard and fast, especially at night in the countryside, then vanishing. (27)

Within a few years, however, the sheer Soviet military superiority and ruthless methods reminiscent of the Nazis took their toll. According to a former colonel with the Soviet Union named Burlitski who later defected to the West, "It was like beating the forests for wild game, except that the game was human. Day after day we formed long lines and combed the forest and swamps, arresting, shooting, burning. If there was any doubt left about escaping from Russia, my experiences in Lithuania put an end to it. Even my well-disciplined soldiers were sickened by their jobs. Often after a particularly grim manhunt I would find them in their quarters half mad with drink; whatever was left of their human feelings was drowned in alcohol." (28)

This observation reminds this writer of similar circumstances regarding the conduct of some American operations in Vietnam, personally related by distraught soldiers during their "rest and recuperation" time in Hawai'i. We have learned of similar atrocities in Iraq. It is a sad and anguishing commentary on the abysmal level of humanity on the part of people who have risen (fallen?) to positions of command over so much of the human race. And without understanding the total irony of their assertions, these very same people are claiming to be "defenders of civilization, freedom, and democracy."

Between 1944 and 1950, eight mass deportations were carried out totaling some 320,000 people. Others were not so "lucky" but were summarily executed. Provocateurs were also employed to commit atrocities while pretending to be resistance fighters. During the same time, the partisan resistance had killed an estimated 100,000 Soviet forces and 4,000 Lithuanian sympathizers. These sacrifices by frantic Lithuanians were predicated on the arrival of military help from the Western Allies which never arrived, leaving countless Lithuanians disillusioned and despairing. (29)

It should be noted, however, that the hopes of the Lithuanian people and their representatives abroad were not merely wishful thinking on their part. They had been given specific encouragement. Consider for example the statement of Sumner Welles, U.S. Undersecretary of State on July 23, 1940:

> During these past few days the devious processes whereunder the political independence and territorial integrity of the three small Baltic Republics—Estonia, Latvia, and Lithuania—were to be deliberately annihilated by one of their more powerful neighbors, have been rapidly drawing to their conclusion. From the day when the people of these republics first gained their independence and democratic form of government, the people of the United States have watched their admirable progress in self-government with deep and sympathetic interest.
>
> The policy of this government is universally known. The people of the United States are opposed to predatory activity no matter whether they are carried on by

> the use of force or the threat of force. They are likewise opposed to any form of intervention on the part of one state, however powerful, in the domestic concerns of another state, however weak. These principles constitute the very foundations upon which the existing relationship between the 21 sovereign republics of the New World rest. (30)

Well, it would be hard to come up with a more hypocritical statement than this! These fine noble words are totally belied by over a century of *U.S. behavior* that blatantly and flagrantly contradicts these assertions. There have been and continue to be literally dozens of examples of U.S. military and political intervention (not withstanding the vigorous opposition of U.S. citizens to the misuse of our resources and lives) in Central and South America, Vietnam, Iraq, and of course, the case discussed in this book, Hawai'i. These actions, amply documented in innumerable books and articles, have been *exactly* "predatory activities" which have been carried out both by force and the threat of force. As we have seen in the case of Hawaiian sovereignty, they employed both.

However, in the Lithuanian case, the non-recognition of Soviet control (part of the foundation of the Cold War between the U.S., representing corporate capitalism, and the U.S.S.R., initially representing socialism but evolving into state capitalism) gave Lithuanians a wedge to use to maintain *de jure* independence and have diplomatic representation in a number of countries. For instance, "During World War II, Great Britain extended de facto recognition of Lithuania's incorporation into the U.S.S.R.. However, the British government refused to accord *de jure* recognition to the annexation." (31) Many other countries followed suit.

Over the next few years a Lithuanian American Council was set up to unite Americans of Lithuanian descent and to press on the diplomatic front for recognition of Lithuania as an independent country, and to disseminate news of their homeland. When a prominent Lithuanian, Dr. Pijus Grigaitis, as part of a small delegation, visited Pres. Franklin Roosevelt and objected to the loss of Lithuanian independence, the latter had these important and encouraging words to say:

> I understand perfectly your feelings concerning the fate of Lithuania. Let me tell you that you have made here two mistakes: the first mistake is in your address that you gave me. It is stated here that Lithuania has lost her independence. It is a mistake to say so. Lithuania did not lose her independence—Lithuania's independence was only temporarily put aside. Time will come and Lithuania will be free again. This will happen sooner than you may expect. The other mistake that I observed was made by one of your speakers when he referred to Lithuania as a very small state. Look at the Latin American Republics and you will see that there are even smaller states than Lithuania, but they live a free and happy life. It is not fitting to even talk about the smallness of Lithuania for even the smallest nation has the same right to enjoy independence as the largest nation. (32)

Replace the name "Lithuania" with "Hawaii" and you have the case for Hawaiian sovereignty in a nutshell. This is **exactly** what activists in Hawai'i are saying, that Hawai'i's nationhood has not vanished, but that her "independence was only temporarily put aside." As stated earlier, there is no statute of limitations on burglarized sovereignty.

On the diplomatic front subsequently, the Government of the Federal Republic of Germany issued a statement that reasoned that "since the annexation of the Baltic States was not recognized in international law and the citizens of those states had not become citizens of the Soviet Union, the citizenship of those persons remained unchanged; hence, passports issued by the diplomatic and consular services of Estonia, Latvia and Lithuania were valid as long as they conformed to the usual regulations." (33)

At the conclusion of WW2 in Europe, the VL IK (Supreme Committee for Liberation of Lithuania) prepared a detailed piece of diplomacy and sent it to the U.S. President and the British Prime Minister. The central provisions were to request that these two nations

> 1) not recognize the unilateral act of the Kremlin which incorporated Lithuania into the Soviet Union, 2) demand that the Soviet Union remove its forces from the country and allow Lithuanians to re-establish without hindrance their sovereign institutions, 3) stipulate that until such time, Lithuanian displaced persons should be sheltered by the Allies, and 4) force the Soviet Union to return all Lithuanians deported to Siberia, the operation to be supervised by the International Red Cross. (34)

History has shown that these demands were not implemented. The VL IK also maintained active correspondence with the United Nations and many other national and international organizations, consistently pressing the case for restoration of sovereignty. (35)

Once military resistance to occupation by the U.S.S.R. was defeated by sheer force of numbers, the effort turned to diplomatic and educational efforts. Radio and publishing news about Lithuania to sympathizers worldwide became a central focus.

On the diplomatic front, this example can be seen as characteristic:

> In 1957, the President of the Supreme Committee, Antanas Trimakas, made a goodwill tour to Brazil,

Uruguay, Argentina, Peru, Bolivia, Venezuela, and Panama. The Conference of Latin American Presidents, which was taking place in Panama at the time, provided Mr. Trimakas with an excellent occasion to meet a number of Latin American leaders. These acquaintances proved to be very useful door-openers to the cabinets, press, and other institutions during subsequent visits to the capitals of the respective countries. During this Latin American tour, the President held over forty press conferences and gave several radio and T.V. talks. (36)

Continuing efforts were made to influence Congressional opinion in the United States. For example, one major effort succeeded in passing on June 23rd, 1966, a resolution in both Houses of Congress encouraging the President to bring the Lithuanian case to the United Nations and other relevant international bodies in a manner that put on the agenda restoration of the right to self-determination for Lithuania, Estonia, and Latvia—all of whom shared the same fate of being absorbed by the U.S.S.R. after WW II. (37) The requirement for a long view of history and the ability of Lithuanian statesmen to achieve this long view can be shown in a couple of passages from this definitive Lithuanian history book, *Lithuania: 700 Years.* During the period of time between the two world wars, when Lithuania had achieved independence and national unity, the nation was at peace at home and with all countries. "One of the rules of Lithuania's foreign policy was that in the event of war much could be lost, while peace would guarantee the future of the nation. One must remember that Lithuania won all of the cases to which she was party to the International Court of Justice at The Hague." (38)

Despite the setback generated by the occupation of Lithuania, this long view of history gives reason for optimism even during the bleakest days. Recalling that this book was published in 1969 at the height of Soviet power, the author states, "The course of nineteenth and twentieth century history bears witness to the fact that the major idea, which cannot be hindered or stopped in its development is that of personal and national freedom. Violations of this idea are mere episodes in the course of history." (39)

When one looks at history, one is struck by the observation that small states do not initiate wars, but strive for peaceful resolutions of conflicts. In our context, Hawai'i as an independent nation never went to war against a single country in nearly a century of its fully expressed sovereignty. It is worth noting that if many small countries worked together jointly for justice and peace, condemning aggressive behavior on the part of more powerful countries, such an effort can inhibit the ambitions of the latter.

The recent example of resistance to the attempt by the U.S.A to conquer Iraq is a case in point. At great financial risk, many small nations refused to align themselves with the doctrine of "pre-emptive war," despite universal abhorrence to the regime of Saddam Hussein. True, they did not succeed in preventing the war, but it was delayed and the U.S. effort was not able to acquire more than token participation by any other country except the United Kingdom, whose population, nonetheless, was overwhelmingly opposed to the scheme.

The recent walkout from the Cancun, Mexico meeting of the World Trade Organization (the notorious front group for global capitalism) is a most encouraging sign of assertion of national sovereignty in the face of pressure from imperial power. In the same category, promotion of smaller nation autonomy came during the recent fair elections in Bolivia, Chile, Venezuela, Nicaragua, and Argentina, and their trend toward cooperation with each other on the basis of mutual benefit rather than dominator-dominated status. Such trends should be encouraged and accelerated. Voluntary cooperation in pursuit of worthy goals of mutual interest must replace conquest, coercion, bribery, and intimidation which have characterized so much of the nineteenth and twentieth centuries.

The book *Lithuania, 700 Years* concludes with this sentence (again, 1969): "The Lithuanian nation is always ready to return to the community of independent nations, from which it still awaits moral and political support in its quest for liberation and freedom." (40) Replace the word "Lithuanian" with "Hawaiian" and the historical parallel is complete.

After several more decades of heavy-handed stifling of the desire for independence on the part of the Lithuanians, a rare opportunity came during the liberalization effort of Mikhail Gorbachev and subsequent disintegration of the mighty U.S.S.R.. It will be instructive to review the final phase that enabled Lithuania to gain its independence after 50 years of "annexation," for its example to Hawaii's similar effort.

The tight grip of authoritarian rule had begun to erode in Eastern Europe during the 70's and 80's and finally the hated symbol of oppression, the Berlin Wall, had been torn down. Lithuanians saw an opportunity to reassert their independence once again. While Lithuanians appreciated Gorbachev's commitment, backed up by his actions, to reduce the oppressive behavior of past administrations, they could not approve his reluctance to grant genuine independence. This reluctance was intimately connected with his own fate as leader and that of the U.S.S.R. itself. Many other eastern European nations were watching keenly the emerging high-stakes confrontation, hoping their turn would be next. (41)

Initially, the broad-based Lithuanian Reconstruction Movement known as Sajudis, mindful of the huge sacrifices made by the previous generation of Lithuanians, intended to avoid heavy handed-repression by utilizing persuasion and negotiation. One of their favorite methods was to use "calendar demonstrations" marking anniversaries of important historical events, such as August 23rd, marking the anniversary of the Molotov-Ribbontrop Pact (otherwise known as the Stalin-Hitler non-aggression treaty). (42) A parallel event exists in Hawai'i with the annual commemoration of the January 17, 1893 overthrow of the Queen. Along the same lines, the 70th anniversary of the Feb. 16th, 1918 Independence Day in 1918 had great significance for Lithuanians in 1988. Not only were those opposed to the U.S.S.R. in principle involved, but many Lithuanian communists as well who aspired to both national independence and an economic system based on socialist principles. (43) Lithuanians living abroad offered both moral and material support by donating fax machines and computers along with money, while lobbying governments in their lands of residence to support the Lithuanian cause. (44)

U.S. trips were arranged and implemented for several people who would play important roles in the successful unarmed uprising to come. Among these were Kazimiera Prunskiene and Vytautas Landsbergis, who would become, respectively, Lithuania's first prime minister and president. Victor Nakas, who ran the Lithuanian Information Center in Washington, D.C. would on occasion make TV appearances in the U.S. and act as translator for Landsbergis for U.S. audiences. (45)

In Lithuania itself,

> The mass demonstrations had a powerful, organic impact upon the vast majority of Lithuanians who had participated in them. A dramatic transformation of consciousness took place as people previously intimidated by the oppressive might of the Soviet state became fearless and ignored threats and concrete displays of force that once had cowed them into demean-

ing silence. (46)

Sajudis was able to unite "highly educated, talented, well-connected leaders who could forge popular but heretofore inchoate protest into organized opposition." (47) During the early stages, it tried to hold two ultimately contradictory positions: remaining within a liberalized U.S.S.R. and repudiating the heavy bureaucracy of past decades while on the other hand pushing hard for ultimate sovereignty. These two aims clashed on Nov. 20, 1988 when Sajudis selected Landsbergis as its president with the announcement that "only Lithuania can decide and execute its laws." (48) On February of the next year, Landsbergis would proclaim that "international recognition of Lithuanian independence is still valid." (49) This, indeed, is the very position held by the most astute of Hawaiian activists today, namely that the status of the *de jure* Hawaiian state remains unchanged, despite a century of occupation.

Reminiscent of the 1960's U.S. draft protestors, (of which this writer was one) young Lithuanian men began to burn draft cards imposed by Soviet occupiers, not only for the purpose of rejected forcible military service to the U.S.S.R., but also to protest the history of abusive treatment of Lithuanian recruits by the Soviet military. (50) Describing his experience at the Independence Day, 1990 celebration, *Showdown* author Richard J. Krikus wrote with emotion:

> I am a political scientist, a third generation Lithuanian American on my father's side of the family, who neither speaks nor reads Lithuanian. I am a well-traveled middle aged man who finds it difficult to get excited about much. I was enthralled! Scenes of crowds descending on the Winter Palace in St. Petersburg in 1917, precipitating the first Russian Revolution, flashed through my mind. The crowd had produced a surge of human energy that was palpable. Everyone in it sensed that they were witnessing a historical event of monumental

dimensions. (51)

That exuberance and spirit reminded Krickus as well of the 1963 March on Washington for civil rights when Martin Luther King gave his famous "I have a Dream" speech. Indeed, Lithuanians were heard saying "We shall overcome!" Speakers called upon the spirits of Thomas Jefferson, Abraham Lincoln, Mahatma Gandhi and Nelson Mandela, as well as King, explaining that the matter transcended mere nationalism and was a demand for human rights. (52)

Upon receiving word of Lithuania's Declaration of Independence on March 11, 1990, the Soviet government acted to force it to be rescinded. Among the measures attempted were conspicuous military maneuvers, an order for Lithuanians to surrender weapons, seizure of a number of schools and government buildings and the printing facilities of major independence-oriented newspapers. Gorbachev then issued a directive for a non-binding referendum, a five year waiting period, with the final decision by the Soviet parliament. (53)

Lithuanians would not buy it. They had come too far and were ready for independence now, on the grounds that "Lithuania had been forcefully incorporated into the U.S.S.R. and therefore was not subject to Soviet law." (54) This is **exactly** the argument made by courageous Hawaiian activists, an argument, which of course, gets no respect in U.S. courts, but does get the courtesy of at least being heard in international venues.

When Lithuania remained adamant, Gorbachev launched an economic embargo to pressure a retreat. That too failed because it solidified the Lithuanian people to resist no matter the sacrifice. Moreover, it spurred sympathizers throughout the U.S.S.R. to offer help to their embattled Lithuanian friends. One result of this standoff was that Boris Yeltsin felt emboldened to begin his challenge to Gorbachev. With the economy of the U.S.S.R., as well as its political foundations in disarray, the leadership could ill-afford to alienate the U.S. and its ample grain reserves. (55) In effect, Gorbachev found himself between the proverbial rock and a hard place with nowhere to turn without a huge sacrifice somewhere else.

Heroes have arisen historically at times of crisis. Lithuania's hero was a soft-spoken professor by the name of Vytautas Landbergis, previously mentioned. As tensions rose between his country and the U.S.S.R., it was proposed that the new president go into voluntary temporary exile. However, Krickus relates,

> With Landsbergis out of the picture, the Lithuanian drive for independence would have disintegrated. He had become the person with whom the Lithuanian people and most steadfast rebels had identified as the leader of their bold drive for independence. . . .But this mild-mannered man, who had accepted Soviet subjugation of his country without protest most of his life refused to surrender and urged his people to stand fast in the face of overwhelming odds. Lawry Wyman, a Harvard lawyer reported, 'I was amazed by Landsbergis's composure. His calm steadfastness had a positive tranquilizing effect upon the Lithuanian population. Landsbergis did not want his people to resort to violence and give the Soviets the pretext to slaughter them.' (56)

Such descriptions bring to mind the similar collective courage a few years earlier in 1986 by the million or more Filipinos who gathered in Manila to demand the resignation of U.S.-backed Philippine dictator Ferdinand Marcos. Students, housewives, clergy, workers and many middle class professional people had declared "Enough!" after the assassination of 50-year old would-be democratic challenger Benigno Aquino at Manila's airport minutes after he had returned from a lengthy stay in the United States, along with the subsequent election in which Marcos had "won" a rigged election against the widow of Aquino, Corazon Aquino. These brave people were rewarded when their sons, brothers, uncles and fathers in the Philippine military forces refused to shoot unarmed people, and Marcos was forced to flee for his life, ironically, to Hawai'i, the subject of this book. It would be interesting to research the topic and see if that event of world historical significance had impacted the consciousness of those who successfully applied the same lesson in Vilnius, Lithuania only four years later.

Realizing that the whole world was watching events unfold on TV no doubt had a restraining influence on Soviet authorities. "Outside of Lithuania, there were two people especially upset about television's coverage of Bloody Sunday—Mikhail Gorbachev and George Bush." (57) For Gorbachev, it is obvious that the less the exposure of a crackdown the better for his efforts to contain the situation. But Bush had just begun a build-up to begin the first U.S. assault on Iraq after the Iraqis had been led to believe that the U.S. would not intervene when Iraqi tanks and soldiers overran Kuwait. Bush was seeking a broad coalition, and the Soviet Union was a central player. Bush was just as eager for cordial relations with Gorbachev as the reverse. (58)

TV coverage of events in Lithuania affected U.S. policies indirectly, which in turn affected the volatile scene in Moscow. President George H. W. Bush was getting pressure from within his own party to provide assistance to the brave Lithuanians. Numerous acts of courage could be found among the thousands who rallied to assert their independence. Faced with guns and even shots into crowds, the latter would respond with patriotic songs. "One can surmise that millions of TV viewers who witnessed this scene from around the world were both awestruck and inspired by this gripping display of bravery." (59)

To this writer, it seems that consciousness of this impact of seeing people engaged in liberating themselves has impacted the view of rulers themselves in many countries. We have witnessed in the time since 1990 a marked increase in assaults upon journalists, including outright assassinations, most specifically in the Middle East where U.S. and Israeli military personnel have reportedly targeted people who were conspicuously reporters. The same has occurred in other countries. Apparently it is not only truth itself which is a casualty of war, but now as well the people trying to report the truth—repression identified as totalitarian conduct by any sane judgment.

Upon completion of a huge victory at this election, many of the Sajudis activists expected a fast recognition of independence by Western powers, especially the U.S. This view, shared by the new president, Landsbergis, was incorrect. The principal reason was that the administration of George H. W. Bush, looking at the interests of the U.S. government, decided that it was more important to maintain good relations with Gorbachev, who had been much more open to negotiations, including nuclear issues, than his predecessors. The superpower relationship took priority over the liberation of the nation of Lithuania. The end of the cold war was at hand and the U.S. could smell victory. They were not about to risk a major setback by having hardliners throw out Gorbachev and impose harsh militaristic rule again in order for a small country to gain independence. But events, were, for the most part, out of U.S. hands. (60)

When a delegation of Lithuanian-Americans got to meet with President Bush on 1/22/91, and Bush would not agree to recognition of Lithuanian independence, one of the delegation exclaimed, "Mr. President, that's appeasement! That's appeasement!" Bush responded by saying indignantly, "Don't use that word!" (61)

Meanwhile, Russian people themselves were learning lessons of their own from this passive revolt:

First lesson: Hard-liners would not allow their positions of power and privilege to be removed without a fight.

Second lesson: the most powerful force of the reformers was the mass of dissatisfied people.

Third lesson: military morale is a matter of vital importance. Both individual soldiers and even commanders had no heart for slaughter of courageous unarmed civilians, and consequently withdrew.

Fourth lesson: morale among the hard-liners themselves was tenuous. Some were beginning to believe that their cause was hopeless. Some defected to the opposition. (62)

The net result was that just as England was forced to recognize the independence of "the colonies" in 1781, and India after WW II, many other colonial powers such as France, Spain, and the Netherlands had to give up control over other people and their lands, and the U.S. attempt to conquer Vietnam was thwarted, so the U.S.S.R. was required by historical developments to recognize Lithuanian independence, which it finally did on Sept. 6, 1991.

When will it be Hawai'i's turn?

Chapter 10

Contemporary Resistance in Hawai'i to the American Empire?

A non-resident of Hawai'i may ask, with some justification, "Well, you certainly have made a good case for restoration of effective sovereignty, but isn't it a moot point? After all, unlike the anti-apartheid struggle in South Africa, or the effort of Palestinians to regain control of the Occupied Territories, or the Northern Ireland battle to win independence from England, we never hear of any uprisings, general strikes, or disruptions of business as usual that would indicate that the issue is anything more than a justified academic exercise! Is there any evidence of significant resistance to the *status quo*?"

"Valid question," I would reply. Let's begin. Given the preponderance of military power by the U.S., everyone recognizes that confronting the U.S. militarily would be suicidal. Lacking such, there is little news coverage on the mainland of the numerous determined confrontations that are peaceful in nature. The corporate media, as usual, is compliant with the interests of mega-corporations, such as the major hotel industries like Sheraton, Hilton, and Marriott and the military presence that occupies so much land in Hawai'i.

I had previously referenced the Hawaiian Renaissance, beginning generally around 1970. At that time, very little of the preceding history and analysis cited in this book was widely known. It was generally accepted that the actions of the U.S. and the local conspirators in the 1890's constituted a historic injustice to the Hawaiian people, and regarded by those who reflected on it as being morally untenable, regrettable, but nevertheless, a fact of life in Hawai'i. What has evolved since then is a profound calling into question the legitimacy through international law, as well as even U.S.

law, of each item of the three-stage *coup d'etat*: "overthrow," "annexation," and "statehood."

How did the effort get from the 1970 primordial consciousness of sovereignty to its present mature state? The principle advancement came through land struggles and efforts to protect important surfing sites from development, the latter led by a WW II veteran and bold radical, as well as very competent surfer, John Kelly, who never refrained from saying that as long as people have correct information, and are unified in their commitment to a just cause, they can win. He and his wife Marion served as political mentors to this writer in the sixties. In both the surf and land questions, the question of "Who benefits?" always came front and center. Thus was an introduction of class struggle and of systematic ethnic discrimination to a new generation of Hawai'i residents of many nationalities. "Why is it that relatively poor but honest people, usually brown-skinned, have to move away so that rich developers, some white and some local also with brown skins, can get richer? Why is resort development regarded as superior to farming, fishing, or the propagation of the Hawai'i-invented form of recreation known as surfing?"

I can recall numerous such struggles to preserve homes and communities during that period, well-known to my generation of people living on Oahu at the time: Kalama Valley (the first), located out by Sandy Beach on the east end of Oahu, Chinatown evictions, and partial fill in of Salt Lake (not the Utah one!) for condo development, Waiahole-Waikane Valleys well known for rich agricultural land and abundant rainfall, Sand Island, Halawa Valley, just to name a few that come to mind so many years later. People on the neighbor islands will have their own recollections.

The more overtly political effort, alluded to earlier (Chapter 8), the focussed drive to get the military to stop bombing Kaho'olawe and return it to Hawaiian control was a central focus from mid-1970's until general victory in the late

1980's. The victory, however, fell short of a the comprehensive clean up of some forty-five years of military hardware, mostly bomb pieces known by the euphemism "ordnance."

Simultaneous with these struggles, a movement on campuses evolved to push for Ethnic Studies classes and full degrees. The slogan, "our history, our way" motivated many dozens of students, distinguishing it from the sanitized versions being taught, ones that ignored or downplayed racism, vehement labor confrontations, and the submerged history of the "annexation" period. People began to connect the physical confrontations with what was being learned with new research material, and it made sense. Some of this awareness evolved into the popular music of the time. Culture, history, music, and personal identity gradually came into focus for uncounted numbers of young people.

In terms of sheer numbers physically present, nothing in contemporary Hawaiian history can match the outpouring that occurred exactly 100 years to the day that the Queen was pressured, under threat of violence, to temporarily surrender to the U.S. As a participant, I can recall the sense of dignity, grim determination, and pride as some 12,000 people, mostly Hawaiian, gathered at Iolani Palace, adjacent to the downtown business area of Honolulu, January 17, 1993. Each year subsequently similar, but far smaller gatherings take place, reinforcing historical knowledge and determination to win back effective sovereignty.

As the research into the history of that fateful period of the 1890's progressed, a few began to examine the legality (or lack thereof) of the U.S. intrusion into the affairs of this small country, and the literal occupation of the limited land mass, from which has to be excluded numerous very steep mountains. Though too steep for human habitation or cultivation, these steep mountains provide a valuable purpose for life by retaining abundant water seeping down through thick vegetation to the underground lava tubes that serve as nature's holding tanks.

During the last forty years, numerous organizations have evolved to promote sovereignty, some with the aim of complete separation from the U.S., and others with more limited aims, believing that total victory is not possible, and willing to settle for what they deem realistic goals. This author's orientation should be obvious to readers, but it is not my *kuleana* (right, responsibility, jurisdiction) to evaluate the various organizational efforts, some based on Hawaiian geneological claims. I will point out, however, that with Hawaiian society, as with all others, there exist class differences. As a general rule, with often major exceptions, the wealthier Hawaiians are more likely to seek some accommodation with U.S. authorities in some sort of power-sharing arrangement.

As the blatant and flagrant violations of both U.S. Constitutional law and international law came to light, activists in Hawai'i began to look at remedies, first through the legal system of the U.S. and its wholly owned subsidiary, "the State of Hawai'i." Finding no justice there, the next step was to go to international organizations, especially the United Nations, where to date they have found a measure of sympathy especially in countries with major populations of indigenous people, but little legal redress from the U.S. which has stonewalled with this rationale: "Since 1959 'statehood,' the matter is settled." This official U.S. position is parroted by corporate media and others serving the interests of the U.S. empire. But of course, armed robbery of effective (*de facto*) sovereignty as opposed to legal (*de jure*) sovereignty) has no statute of limitations, as mentioned earlier. The case of Lithuania is exhibit "A" in that regard.

The effort to achieve effective sovereignty has two main thrusts: 1) the ongoing resistance to ever-more control as played out in land and water mobilizations, and 2) historical revelations which have evolved into sophisticated arguments based on international law.

A recent dramatic manifestation of the former is the

determined and successful effort to prevent deployment of the Superferry, ostensibly for civilian use inter-island, but with a more sinister purpose lurking just beneath the surface, like a great white shark preparing to devastate his surface prey. A remarkable book called *Superferry Chronicles: Hawaii's Uprising Against Militarism, Commercialism, and the Desecration of the Earth* documents this effort's drama.

On August 16, 2007, the 351-foot long Superferry, burning 6000 gallons of diesel fuel with four underwater jet engines traveled from Honolulu on its maiden voyage and attempted to enter Nawiliwili Harbor (the major harbor on Kaua'i), despite overwhelming prior protests and a 5-0 Hawai'i Supreme Court order prohibiting deployment before an full Environmental Impact Statement (EIS) was performed. With blade-like pontoons and traveling at 40 MPH, this huge catamaran had the potential to devastate the many species of whale, porpoise, dolphin and turtle populations which are abundant in Hawaiian waters. In addition, the prospect of large-scale pollution from the engines, transmittal of invasive species, not only from the ship itself, but from the hundreds of automobiles and its passengers it was intended to carry daily, and just plain intrusiveness into the rural, peaceful, lightly populated lifestyle of Kaua'i made it highly unwelcome.(1) From the book's authors' narration, here's what happened next at Nawiliwili Harbor:

"So, when we saw this gigantic catamaran enter the harbor, specifically sized to transport heavy military vehicles (as we later discovered), racing headlong toward us in flagrant disregard of all our efforts, we were outraged. About 1,500 of us *spontaneously* gathered at the dock to try once again to make clear what our state officials had refused to hear: We would not allow this luxury monstrosity on our shores until an EIS had been satisfactorily completed. We chanted, sang, and beat drums. We brandished banners and waved ti leaves, the sacred plant that wards off evil while calling in the good.

"In that moment, all remnants of the old sugar-era manipulations that had pitted race against race, class against class, vanished. Shoulder-to-shoulder stood Native Hawaiians; Japanese-, Filipino-, Portuguese-, and Chinese-American descendants of plantation workers; descendants of American missionaries; and transplants from North America who have been calling Kaua'i home for as long as forty years and as short as six months. Lawyers, musicians, small farmers, students, doctors, college professors, politicians, writers, New Age haoles, woodworkers, social workers, nurses, mechanics, architects—every part of Kauai's community was represented.

"The coup de grace came from a few dozen surfers who suddenly leaped from the jetty's rocky edge to paddle out toward the mouth of Nawiliwili Harbor. Most were kids. There they sat, straddling their boards, looking as small as mice, in comparison to the skyscraper-high ship, yet they blocked it from moving forward—a sort of Tiananmen Square challenge in the waters of Kaua'i! It was dangerous; they went right up under the bow of the mammoth boat. Then dozens more swimmers jumped into the water, some with boogie boards, and headed out toward the ship, despite the strident warnings from officials in Coast Guard and police boats. No one was killed, but they could have been." (2)

After a couple of hours, and with the support of a SWAT team, the Superferry was able to gingerly proceed and disembark the unwelcome passengers.

"THE NEXT EVENING, the vessel returned, and the number of people in the water doubled. Protesters in kayaks and traditional Hawaiian outrigger canoes joined those on surfboards to form a human blockade, Onshore were SWAT teams from O'ahu holding back German shepherds. A handful of arrests were made, which included four children, but they could not clear away the citizens in the water. After three hours, the boat was forced to back out of the harbor and return to O'ahu. . . .The Superferry has not returned to Kaua'i since." (3)

Why did this happen? Apparently, it was the proverbial straw that broke the camel's back, as simmering resentment had been built for decades, like magma under the Hawaiian island chain, until finally an eruption occurs.

"By the time the Superferry showed up, displaying its own high degree of entitlement and ignorance of local concerns, it was seen as a foreign monster, a prime example of corporate soullessness that may not have been unique in Hawaiian history, but had arrived at the wrong moment. The people knew what to do. The mood of the island shifted. It marked the turning point of consciousness, political will, and self-determination. The citizens of Kaua'i were transformed." (4)

The corporate media, in their usual behavior, scoffed at the protest movement and tried to marginalize the protesters as uninformed and insignificant. The people knew better. It was the media who were simply "not getting it."

"Three weeks later after the events in Nawiliwili Harbor, there was a third fateful date. That was Sept. 20, 2007, when Governor Lingle made her one greatest mistake, rooted in her own blind arrogance, by descending upon Kaua'i to declare that her decisions were final, and to threaten the protesters with fines and imprisonment. The people were outraged, and poured forth three hours of eloquent testimonies . . ." (5)

Arriving at the county building auditorium with the intent to proclaim an ultimatum, blindly intent on pursuing the Superferry with its military baggage at any cost, she stepped into a hornets nest of protest. "She had come to tell us, in no uncertain terms, that the Superferry *would* return to Kaua'i, and when it did, we would not be allowed within a large, newly designated 'security zone.' Anyone violating these new boundaries would be subject to arrest under federal antiterrorism law, carrying a fine of up to $10,000 and imprisonment up to ten years." (6)

Yet in the wonderful spirit of Hawaiian *onipa'a* (being steadfast), that arrogance was confronted and smashed. "What instead unfolded was a dramatic reversal of roles—instead of the governor speaking *down* to her subjects, it was the people speaking powerfully to her—in a cavalcade of brilliant, heartfelt oratory. . . . in passionate defense of their 'aina, of their civil rights, of marine life, and of the island's rural soul." (7)

Here are a few excerpts of the testimony:

Gov. Lingle: " 'We're not here tonight to make a decision about when the Superferry comes in, because we've made that decision already.'

(The audience bursts into a rumble of discontent, punctuated by angry heckling.)" (8)

Then Gov. Lingle addressed the concern of many that the Superferry was connected to ever more military build up beyond the near saturation point already. " 'I don't know of any issue that the Superferry has to do with national security.' *(The crowd boos loudly),"* (9) clearly in disbelief at this brazen distortion of reality, when the major players are tightly bound up with military contracts, and in particular as a transport for the massive Stryker tanks.

The utter arrogance of Gov. Lingle's approach, and absolute rejection of traditional aloha spirit was well documented by the testimony of one of the early speakers, a recent (2002) resident with 22 years in law enforcement, recently retired, Rich Hoeppner. He reported that he had been deeply offended by the blatant rejection of the democratic process, and had circulated a petition to require an EIS, easily getting 6000 signatures over a few months from citizens of lightly populated Kaua'i (total population around 60,000).

He had taken the petitions to the Capitol in Honolulu and proceeded respectfully through the appropriate protocol, but had been rebuffed at every step. Gov. Lingle had refused to come to a meeting to discuss the matter, and then, when a small delegation went to her office, neither she nor any of her subordinates agreed to either meet him or accept the petitions. Completing his testimony in the auditorium, Hoeppner announced to the enthusiastic crowd, "I have those petitions tonight." He delivered them to her in view of the audience and then, in reference to her refusal to obey the Supreme Court's emphatic ruling, " 'If you were in consort with the Superferry to violate State law, is that an impeachable offense?' *(The word impeachment elicits squeals from the audience.)*" (10)

Another speaker, Lloyd Imuaikaika Pratt, one of Kauai'i's most eminent practitioners of Hawaiian culture and spirituality, said, in part, "I am a native of this land; my ancestors go way back, six centuries and back. And here you guys are making decisions for us when you don't even live here. . . .We speak full *mana* (supernatural power) to you folks, and we try to make you listen to us. Because we are the one who is affected by it. But yet, you fraudulent people who are here as government, which is actually fictitious here, in our homelands, and trying to tell us that this is this, when actually it's all fictitious." (11) He was no doubt referring to the subject matter of this book, the illegitimacy of U.S. and "State" laws.

Another Native Hawaiian, Robert Pa, a master canoe builder with a list of credentials to his name, spoke in opposition as well, concluding . . . " 'the first whale comes on the beach killed from that boat, I'm going to drag it to (mayor of Kaua'i) Bryan Baptiste's office!' *(An incredulous roar bursts from the crowd.)* . . . 'We're taking this further, and we're taking it to the top. And it ain't the State of Hawai'i. And your capitalism.' " (12)

Raymond Catania said, in part: "For all my life, I've seen nothing but development and destruction happening every day. And I tell you what—this is the first time that I have ever seen Child Welfare Services, which is a good agency to help with child abuse, being used against the people of Kaua'i because we standing up!" (referring to the threat to parents of children who took part in the shoreline demonstrations). "*(The auditorium roars in support.)* 'I can say this, because I WORK IN CHILD WELFARE SERVICES!' *(Seemingly impossible, the crowd cheers even more loudly.)*" (13)

These few statements, among many more, give the reader a feel for what occurred. The good news is—they won! The Superferrry is gone, not only from Kaua'i, but from all Hawaiian waters. Lingle's term expired in 2010 and multiple-term Democratic Congressman and long ago political activist Neil Abercrombie was inaugurated as Governor in December, 2010. Although contemporary activists have been disappointed in his performance, such an evaluation is beyond the scope of this work.

In addition to the big generic question of burglary of effective sovereignty, a more tangible immediate question of validity of land titles has come into perspective. I use the term "burglary" rather than "theft" for a reason. "Theft" has connotations of "shoplifting," taking something and escaping without being noticed. "Burglary," however, is far more aggressive in its connotations, a brazen taking by force or threat of force, in full sight of the owner, as in "armed robbery." This seems applicable to Hawai'i's experience. Without the aggressive posture of U.S. troops from the *U.S.S. Boston*, the assault on the integrity of Hawai'i's government would not have succeeded, nor even been undertaken.

In a surprising turnaround, and in view of the "Apology Law" (Appendix B) known as UNITED STATES PUBLIC LAW 103-50, signed by President Clinton, the Hawai'i Supreme Court on January 31, 2008, put a cloud over the title of the "ceded lands" by declaring that the "State" cannot sell or otherwise transfer these lands. The "ceded lands" were those which had, prior to "annexation," belonged to the legitimate government of Hawai'i or to the monarchy as personal property, called "Crown Lands."

The Apology Bill clearly acknowledged this historic truth, namely that there was no legal justification for the blatant U.S. backed intrusion into the sovereign affairs of a friendly country. If, in fact, such intrusion was illegal (patently so), then the later "transfer" of title to those lands has no validity. One cannot sell, give or convey land one does not own! Again, the common analogy of "selling" the Brooklyn Bridge comes to mind. The Hawai'i Supreme Court ruling threw the "State" and its ruling class into panic mode. It promptly appealed to the U.S. Supreme Court.

Within the context of this book, such an appeal is irrelevant, since the authority of the U.S. Supreme Court stops at the borders of the United States. To continue with my earlier analogy, it has no authority over affairs in Denmark. But in the context of everyday reality, with the U.S. in effective control, it would have great relevance to all who today claim any portion of this vast tract of land. As described by Leon Siu, whose position on October 1, 2008 as cited in his paper on this topic (COMMENTARY ON THE HAWAII CEDED LANDS CASE AT THE U.S. SUPREME COURT) is that of "Minister of Foreign Affairs for Ke Aupuni O Hawaii, the Hawaiian Kingdom."

"While it is true that the State of Hawaii does not own the 'ceded lands' neither do the so-called 'native Hawaiians.'

"By citing 'native Hawaiians' as the default claimants to the 'ceded lands' the State Supreme Court perpetuates a critical error, ignoring the historical and lawful fact that the lands in question belong to the Hawaiian Kingdom, not the 'native Hawaiians.'

"This misdirection is employed to avoid addressing the actual crime—the theft of the national autonomy and the national lands of the Hawaiian Kingdom. It also avoids the rightful remedy—the return of the national autonomy and national lands to the Hawaiian Kingdom.

"The rightful owners of the land are the parties from

whom they were stolen: the crown (ruling monarch) and the government of the Hawaiian Kingdom. The monarch and the national government hold these lands in trust to benefit the people of Hawaii.

"By projecting the 'native Hawaiian' as the injured party, the State Supreme Court follows the lead of the Apology Law and deliberately misdirects the issue, framing it as a mere domestic problem rather than a significant international violation. . . . .Today, the State of Hawaii perpetuates the fraud in order to cover up its inherent illegitimacy as a puppet government installed under the illegal occupation of the U.S. This 'ceded lands' case represents a desperate effort by the State of Hawaii and the lack of clear title to the so-called 'ceded lands'—officially implicated in the Apology Law as lands having been stolen from the Hawaiian Kingdom.

"The State of Hawaii is counting on the U.S. Supreme Court to: 1) ignore the fact that the lands claimed by the State is (sic) actually stolen property and 2) somehow remove the cloud over the state's claim to these lands. The State's primary obstacle is the Apology Law. Thus, to overcome this obstacle, the state of Hawaii is seeking to have the U.S. Supreme Court dismiss or otherwise invalidate the Apology Law; to render it as a noble sentiment, but having no force of law. Failure to convince the U.S. Supreme Court to nullify the Apology Law would destroy the very basis of the existence of the State of Hawaii. If the Hawaii Supreme Court ruling is upheld, it implies that the State of Hawaii has no land! No land, no State." (14)

As stated earlier, it was only under extreme duress from forces of the U.S. military colluding with a handful of non-native Hawai'i residents that led Queen Lili'uokalani to grant conditional and temporary executive authority to the United States, not to the band of insurrectionists. She anticipated being fully restored to the lawful position as Queen and executive.

With the investigation by Rep. Blount completed, and in subsequent negotiations with President Cleveland that she should be restored, she agreed reluctantly, for the well being of the people, to grant full amnesty to those who had carried out the *coup d'etat.* That this state of affairs was mutually understood can be verified by the statement of the then Secretary of State Walter Gresham: "The Government of Hawaii surrendered its authority under a threat of war, until such time only as the Government of the United states, upon the facts being presented to it, should reinstate the constitutional sovereign." (15) A similar statement by President Cleveland removes any doubt whatsoever about the conditional and temporary surrender to avoid armed conflict.

The wording of the directions from Sec. of State Gresham to his negotiator, U.S. Minister Plenipotentiary Albert Willis is as follows, in part:

" 'You will, however, at the same time inform the Queen that, when reinstated, the President expects that she will pursue a magnanimous course by granting full amnesty to all who participated in the movement against her, including persons who are, or have been, officially or otherwise, connected with the Provisional government, depriving them of no right or privilege which they enjoyed before the so-called revolution. All obligations created by the Provisional Government in due course of administration should be assumed.

" 'Having secured the Queen's agreement to pursue this wise and humane policy, which it is believed you will speedily obtain, you will then advise the executive of the Provisional Government and his ministers of the President's determination of the question which their action and that of the Queen devolved upon him, and that they are expected to promptly relinquish to her constitutional authority.' " (16)

The initial response of the Queen was to assert that the conspirators " 'were the cause of the revolution and the constitution of 1887 (The Bayonet Constitution—author). There will never be any peace while they are here. They must be sent out of the country, or punished, and their property confiscated.' " (17)

This position put a halt to the process of restoration. The U.S. position, via President Cleveland, reaffirmed that unless she concurred, the U.S. would not act on her behalf, implying that if she did concede the point, the full weight of the U.S. government would come to bear on her behalf, and against the usurpers, with the cautionary note that U.S. law required Congressional authority to use force. (18)

Faced with the alternatives of non-help from the U.S. government, the Queen reluctantly agreed to the onerous terms. However, help from the U.S. government never materialized, even from the sympathetic administration of Grover Cleveland. His successor, William McKinley, had little sympathy, or it seems, comprehension of the legal issues, and became an ardent supporter of annexation.

Nevertheless, these executive agreements, signed in good faith by both sides continue to bind the U.S. government to honor its part of the bargain, namely to restore to power the successor to the Queen, whoever that may be. In short, until it has complied with these agreements, the U.S. is precluded from asserting claims such as:

1. Recognition of any pretended government other than the Hawaiian Kingdom as the lawful government of the Hawaiian Islands;

2. Annexation of the Hawaiian Islands by joint resolution in 1898;

3. Establishment of a U.S. territorial government in 1900;

4. Administration of the Hawaiian Islands as a non self-governing territory since 1898 pursuant to Article 73(e) of the UN Charter;

5. Admission of Hawai'i as a State of the Federal Union in 1959; and,

6. Designating Native Hawaiians as an indigenous people

situated within the United States with a right to self-determination. (19)

Further, the U.S. "may not rely on the provisions of its internal law as justification for failure to comply with its obligation." (20)

According to a press release dated 6/1/2010, "Dr. David Keanu Sai, a national of the Hawaiian Kingdom, today filed a complaint in Federal Court in Washington, DC against U.S. President Obama, U.S. Secretary of State Clinton, U.S. Secretary of Defense Gates, U.S. Pacific Command Commander Admiral Willard and Hawai'i Governor Lingle for violation of an 1893 Agreement between the United States and the Hawaiian Kingdom and is seeking punitive damages of $10 million for malicious indictment, prosecution, and conviction of a so-called felony. The Defendants have 60 days from the date of service to file an answer to the complaint." (21)

Dr. Sai asserts standing under Title 28, United States Code #1350, " 'alien's action for tort,' for maliciously prosecuting and convicting Dr. Sai for complying with Hawaiian Kingdom law, whereby the prosecution and conviction were violations of the *Lili'uokalani assignment*; the 1907 Hague Convention, IV, and the 1949 Geneva Convention, IV." Further, the suit seeks a permanent injunction, including punitive damages, disgorgement and restitution, to prevent and remedy any violations of the *Lili'uokalani assignment* and the international laws of occupation." (22)

Dr. Sai's doctoral dissertation concerns the very subject matter of this book. He was also the lead agent in the international proceedings (*Larsen vs Hawaiian Kingdom*) at the Permanent Court of Arbitration at The Hague, Netherlands (1999-2001). He has written numerous articles and has given many oral presentations on this subject, including a lengthy period engaging the issue on a weekly two-hour radio program in Honolulu (a series which helped inform this author).

"In the Federal complaint filed today, Dr. Sai alleges the violation of an executive agreement entered into between Queen Lili'uokalani of the Hawaiian Kingdom and President Grover Cleveland of the United States in 1893 . . . .This executive agreement, known as the *Lili'uokalani assignment* (January 17, 1893) was assigned under the threat of war, and binds President Cleveland's successors in office in the administration of Hawaiian Kingdom law until such time as the Hawaiian Kingdom government has been restored in accordance with a second executive agreement between the Queen and President, known as *the Agreement of restoration* (December 18, 1893) whereupon the executive power would be returned and the Hawaiian Kingdom would grant amnesty to those individuals who participated or supported the 1893 insurrection." (23)

Citing legal precedents, Dr. Sai asserts that unlike treaties, executive agreements do not require Senate confirmation. "According to the complaint, the United States misrepresented Hawai'i to be part of the United States since the Spanish–American War by enacting Congressional laws claiming to have annexed the Hawaiian Islands in 1898; to have established the Territory of Hawai'i in 1900; and to have transformed the Territory of Hawai'i into the State of Hawai'i in 1959. The complaint alleges that these actions by Congress are in direct violation of the 1893 executive agreements, and that the Congress has no force and effect beyond U.S. territory." (24)

"Among the alleged misrepresentations that the United States made to the international community:

*That the sovereignty of the Hawaiian Islands was lawfully ceded to the United States by a treaty of cession in 1898;
*That the international treaties between the Hawaiian Kingdom and other sovereign States were superceded by the

United States' treaties with those States;
*That the United States laws and not Hawaiian Kingdom laws governed the Hawaiian Islands to include taxation, tariffs and duties; and
*That the Hawaiian Islands is the territory of the United States through the State of Hawai'i and not the Hawaiian Kingdom, being a sovereign State, which has been under prolonged occupation since the Spanish American War." (25)

"The complaint seeks a permanent injunction, including punitive damages, disgorgement and restitution, to prevent and remedy any violations of the *Lili'uokalani assignment* and the international laws of occupation." (26)

Clearly the matter of true sovereignty for Hawai'i is far from moot, and that like the apparent calm of an ocean when the wind is still, there is a great deal of activity beneath the surface.

Chapter 11

As the Empire Crumbles

If full sovereignty for Hawai'i is to be realized against an adamant and enormously powerful superpower, where do we go from here? The reasonable assumption that it makes no sense to launch a military attack against U.S. forces in Hawai'i should be a no-brainer starting point. (Such a stand would also be a reaffirmation of the actions of the Queen who clearly recognized the futility of such an effort.) But what else does make sense?

The first thing is to realize that all empires crumble in time, and they rarely last more than two or three centuries. It seems clear to huge numbers of people worldwide that the United States government, with its increasingly reckless policies in the fields of military deployment, environmental degradation, cultural insensitivities, and consistent arrogance that would be comical if it were not so dangerous, may be living on borrowed time. In our own lifetime (anyone over twenty-five) we have seen the abrupt end to another empire—that of the Soviet Union, which virtually no one would have predicted even five years earlier. The British empire was effectively ended by WW II, as was that of France. The Spanish empire was gone just as quickly at the beginning of the twentieth century. We must learn, and then teach, that the U.S. cannot, for reasons explained in innumerable other works, maintain such dominance much longer. Nature herself won't allow for such a voracious system of resource waste.

An interesting phenomenon is going on at the northeastern corner of the U.S. which bears on this subject as well. Little Vermont, with a population about half that of Hawai'i, has an active secession movement. In common with Hawai'i,

Vermont was once its own sovereign country, from 1777 to 1791, before joining the United States. Now, for a host of reasons cited below, activists there are attempting to establish the Second Vermont Republic (reference: www.vermontrepublic.org). While Hawai'i has its own historical agenda, Vermont and Hawai'i have *motivations* in common to achieve independence. Here's what Second Vermont Republic's founder, the late Prof. Emeritus Thomas Naylor had to say, in part:

> First, we find it increasingly difficult to protect ourselves from the debilitating effects of big government, big business, big markets, and big agriculture, who want all of us to be the same—just like they are.
>
> Second, in addition to being too big, our government is too centralized, too powerful, too intrusive, too materialistic, and too unresponsive to the needs of individual citizens and small communities.
>
> Third, The U.S. government has lost its moral authority because it is owned, operated, and controlled by Corporate America. National and Congressional elections are bought and sold to the highest bidders.
>
> Fourth, we have a single political party, the Republican Party, disguised as a two-party system. The Democratic Party is effectively brain dead, having had no new ideas since the 1960s.
>
> Fifth, we have become disillusioned with the so-called American way—corporate greed, the war on terrorism, homeland security, the denial of civil liberties, pandering to the rich and powerful, environmental insensitivity and the culture of deceit.

> Sixth, American foreign policy, which is based on the doctrine of *full spectrum dominance,* is immoral, illegal, unconstitutional, and in violation of the United Nations Charter.
>
> Seventh, as long as Vermont remains in the Union, we face the risk of terrorist attack and military conscription of our youth.
>
> Eighth, the U.S. suffers from *imperial overstretch,* and has become unsustainable politically, economically, agriculturally, socially, culturally, and environmentally. It is also ungovernable and unfixable. . . . . (1)

The huge upsurge of left-center parties and governments in Latin America and the quagmires for the United States of Iraq and Afghanistan are clear examples that the empire is in big trouble. Despite the greatest military force the world has ever assembled, the guardians of the empire are finding that not all conflicts have military solutions. They are finding that imperial dictatorship masquerading as democracy does not fly. People are rightly demanding that the resources of their countries ought to be used to benefit the people of those countries, not multi-national corporations who have no allegiance except for the financial bottom line.

Other countries are increasingly disgusted with U.S. government policies and arrogant attitudes from both major political parties, which are correctly seen as mere factions of a single party of empire. The example of Lithuania looms large—when the time is right and the people are united, victory can be won! That is the bottom line. Hawai'i, however, unlike Lithuania, is ethnically diverse to the extreme. Large numbers of Hawaiians are clear that the present system is fundamentally opposed to their interests, and many favor full sovereignty. Others, accepting the premise of a permanent U.S. presence, think the best they can achieve is relative sovereignty, a "nation within a nation" including a definite land base, reparations for the injustice done, and the right to relative autonomy, while leaving the U.S. infrastructure and economic system in place.

To this writer, this latter view, the "nation within a nation" concept, while attempting to secure near-term relief from totally legitimate grievances, concedes far too much. This perspective amounts to begging for a reservation, in the mode of "Indian reservation," which as readers know, has relegated Native Americans to the status of "wards" of the U.S. government, in none but trivial ways "sovereign." If this perspective were applied to Hawai'i, U.S. military bases would remain, the State government would remain, federal laws and U.S. "national interests" would always supersede local laws at the whim of the President or Congress, and so on. This is a recipe for surrender of hope, honor, and national pride, despite temporary and nominal financial and political gain.

At the present time, Hawaiians themselves as a whole are not unified about a path to liberation. Far worse, among other major ethnicities, the Japanese, Chinese, Filipinos, Caucasians, Koreans, Samoans, the issue of sovereignty, for the most part, is seen as an exclusively Native Hawaiian issue, with each person either regarding it at best, either with sympathy and compassion in view of the historic injustice, or at worst, with fear and suspicion—fear that Hawaiians' gain would be their loss. Part of the reason for this perception rests with some pro-sovereignty people who have defined it that way. This perspective, which also showed up during the upsurge of black nationalism, is called "narrow nationalism," in which one's own race is seen as paramount, and people are judged by their lineage and not their deeds or their character.

There is much work to be done. It is imperative that all ethnicities see that true sovereignty, as opposed to the "fake" sovereignty of "reservations," is in their long term self-interest. Of course, the forces of imperialism will do their utmost to divide and conquer, as they always do, playing on ethnic fears. If they succeed when crunch time comes, Hawai'i could become another Bosnia or Iraq with neighbors turning against each other in fury and fear. It is imperative that pre-education be done to avoid slaughter of aloha.

It is important to understand and differentiate between nationality and ethnicity, two terms often used interchangeably in Hawai'i. In a strict legal sense, one's nationality is defined by the country to whom one pays national taxes, the country that would issue your passport, the country who can claim you as its citizen. So, unlike ethnicity, which is a matter of culture, language, and food preferences, among other issues, nationality can change in a single day by becoming a citizen of another country. If a Filipino person comes to the U. S. as an adult, for instance, having been born and raised in the Philippines, that person remains a Filipino ethnically. Likewise, his or her nationality, remains Filipino. However, if that person later accepts and is granted U.S. citizenship, his or her *nationality* changes to that of U.S. (or American). Complicating the matter still further is the matter of race. Consider a person born to second-generation Japanese parents living in San Francisco. By biology, the person is Japanese; by nationality, the person is American (or U.S. citizen); by ethnicity the person is likely a combination of both, probably speaking English as a first language, being more comfortable socially in a San Francisco context than in Tokyo.

When it comes to Hawai'i, the situation becomes even more complex. Consider a third-generation Japanese person as an example, that person may think of him or herself not primarily as an American, but a *person from Hawai'i,* his/her real home, for lack of another term, a local person. In most countries, one would call such a person by their country of birth, e.g., French, German, Danish, and so on. But if you were to speak of such a person as Hawaiian, this would not communicate correctly because in Hawai'i "Hawaiian" refers to ethnicity and biology. If such a person were to travel to a foreign country and were asked "Where are you from?" Such a person would no doubt respond "Hawai'i," not "America" or the "United States," unlike someone from Iowa or Michigan for example.

This sense of identity with Hawai'i is broader and deeper than most mainlanders would expect. Students from Hawai'i seek each other out when attending mainland U.S. colleges for this very reason. This phenomenon is also part of the basis for nationhood that transcends that of Hawaiians alone and must be cultivated and nurtured. All people born and raised in Hawai'i are "Keiki o ka aina," (children of the land) and must be made to feel a part of the *renewal of Hawaiian sovereignty*. As people become increasingly alienated from "the American way of life" with its corporate greed and militaristic and belligerent foreign policies, this feeling of pride in Hawai'i provides a powerful resource upon which to draw in support of sovereignty. In the view of this writer, the term "Hawai'i national" should be introduced to describe people of all ethnicities for whom Hawai'i is truly home and who identify with this struggle for full sovereignty. It might be useful to popularize the term.

Yet another manifestation is the genuine national pride when someone from Hawai'i excels in their field—professional athletes at the highest level, for instance, or when the Ewa Beach and Waipahu Little League teams won world championships in 2005 and 2008. This pride is at a gut level and does not require any knowledge of sovereignty. What is needed from ethnic non-Hawaiians is an evolving consciousness about and commitment to national sovereignty, along with an eagerness to work with Hawaiians who have taken the lead on this issue. The other side of the coin is that Hawaiians must reach out to other ethnic groups in a broad way to make it clear that sovereignty is not just a "Hawaiian" issue, but one that profoundly affects all who live in Hawai'i and those many who would like to return if the economy were not so manipulated and the cost of living so exhorbitant.

There exist within the sovereignty movement *two important and yet distinct valid issues.* The *first* is the subject matter of this book: the armed robbery of Hawai'i's sovereignty and Hawai'i's relationship to other nations of the world, and in particular, the United States. The *other issue*, closely related, is the matter of the historic theft of land and other property, along with non-tangible theft of dignity and respect over many decades perpetuated against indigenous Hawaiians, individually and collectively. By addressing the former, we can create the conditions where the latter can be handled far more deeply and broadly than under any U.S. administration. Such an approach may include as options the setting aside of large tracts of land, even to the extent of entire islands, for use by Hawaiians collectively as a form of regional autonomy. With real sovereignty as the context, such a proposal can proceed from position of strength, not one of supplication.

There are several island nations in the Pacific whose population base and resources are far less than that of Hawai'i: Fiji, Tonga, Samoa, Federated States of Micronesia, just to name a few. The people of Hawai'i will be better off in the long run despite short-term dislocations by becoming independent. When Hawai'i can reestablish her true independence, the presence of U.S. bases will no longer provide a target for nuclear attack nor terrorist sabotage. Someone will of course object, "But what about the jobs the military provides?" A valid question, of course, but answerable. The other side of the coin to the money paid out through military contracts and direct salaries to individuals is the value of one-fourth of the area of Oahu, along with the potential to create more jobs and a far more sustainable economy. Then there are the bases on other islands, including the huge Pohakuloa Training Area on the Big Island. What is the land value and potential of 25% of Oahu? What is the value of a radiation-free future? The submarines that dock at Pearl Harbor are not carrying lollipops for children! What is the value of getting all other weapons of mass destruction out of Hawai'i? What is the value of being able to purge from the school system the poisonous culture that worships warships and state-sponsored violence, i.e. warfare?

What is sovereignty, anyway? Sovereignty is closely related to but is not synonymous with self-determination. One can speak of a sovereign state when it has achieved autonomy, when it is not directly impeded by the authority of another state, and it has the supreme legal authority to deny intrusions from other states. Self-determination for a government is the ongoing exercise of sovereignty and is also the precondition for sovereignty. If self-determination does not exist (as in the 13 colonies in 1775, for instance) then sovereignty does not yet exist.

On a personal level, self-determination means that each person gets to decide important issues. It is the polar opposite of personal slavery. From a societal perspective, self-determination is a collective expression of territoriality, analogous to that found in almost all animals: fish, reptiles, birds and mammals. It appears to be a universal phenomenon that one who inhabits an area "stakes a claim" to it as home and will fiercely defend it against deliberate or inadvertent "invaders." This behavior is seen among animals and from before recorded history among humans. In science fiction, writers project the same kind of values, writing about beings from "outer space" invading "our" space. This view is deep seated.

Self-determination is opposed to servitude, slavery, colonization, occupation, or conquest, whether by nationality, race, sex, or class. Throughout history, there have been abundant examples of people struggling to achieve self-determination *against* another people, who may be neighbors, foreign invaders, an intra-family dominator, class exploiters, etc. In the contemporary era, *virtually all forms of societal denial of self-determination reflect class domination*, not simply bosses vs workers, but privileged position vs underprivileged, and imperialist countries vs underdeveloped countries. This domination is often compounded by virulent racism, sometimes subtle, sometimes overt and vicious. Sovereignty is the autonomous collective agreement to form a self-governing society.

Self-determination is the prerequisite for sovereignty, but is not the same. For example, pre-contact Hawaiians truly exercised self-determination (they were not subject to any other people), but since there was no unified Hawaiian government, one cannot strictly refer to their society as a sovereign nation. Sovereignty denotes supreme authority in a society that is not extinguished by invasion or occupation. So, for instance, when the U.S. occupied post WW II Japan, Japan's sovereignty remained intact. With the overthrow and subsequent occupation, with its falsely claimed "annexation," Hawaiian society lost its self-determination, *but* due to careful application of diplomatic protocols, *not its sovereignty*, which has been dormant for over 100 years. The issue is *under what conditions* can actual functioning self-determination, that is, the exercise of sovereignty, be reestablished.

In the process of obtaining political self-determination, Hawai'i must not neglect economic self-determination as well, for formal independence without obtaining economic independence will lead to a continued dependence on a foreign power for jobs, material goods and even food itself, a condition which would seriously erode the very political independence being sought. A radical break has to be made with the economic order that binds oppressed nation to oppressor nation. In this regard, it is imperative to build alliances with many other nations for trade on the basis of equality, while striving for self-sufficiency in every area where feasible, and especially with respect to energy sources. Fortunately, Hawai'i has an abundance of sunshine, wind, and ocean movement upon which to draw. This author was actively involved with the solar energy business in Hawai'i for nearly twenty years, and can say with assurance, that despite close to one hundred thousand solar water heating systems in place, the potential of solar energy is barely tapped.

The great liberation document signed in 1776 states eloquently that governments derive "their just powers from the consent of the governed." It further adds that when any government becomes destructive of the goals commonly agreed upon when the government was set up, the people have the right to **alter or abolish** such a government. Let us ponder this.

After sixty years of heavy-handed indoctrination on the virtues of (and the impossibility of resistance to) "The American Way," *the fix was in* regarding "statehood." Even the most liberal viewpoint of the day was persuaded that becoming "part of" the United States with formal equality with other states, was a step ahead and would best protect Hawai'i from external enemies. In retrospect, this is sort of like persuading the gopher to become "part of" the rattlesnake to avoid attacks from coyotes, wolves, and eagles. The liberals of that day aimed too low, just as they do today if they limit demands to "reparations," or plead for "a separate land base" *yet within the structure of U.S. jurisdiction.* I hasten to add that reparations and a land base are justified demands on the system, but should not be the strategic end.

We know, of course, that in 1959, the U.S. would not have willingly "granted independence," but a firm demand for a plebiscite on independence might have led to a strategic stalemate leading to a recognition of the legal reality of pre-existing sovereignty, and prevented some of the rampant abuse of resources so evident in Hawai'i today. Looking back to 1776, the most advanced people were asserting not only that it was desirable, but also *possible* for people to break away from an empire and establish an independent identity. The task is very similar today. The first task is to show that it is desirable to do so, then that it is possible.

What would be attractive about independence for both Hawaiians and non-Hawaiian residents of Hawai'i? I have already discussed the goal of getting the occupation military forces out and the huge land area that would be returned. But imagine the unrestrained joy at finding out that citizens of Hawai'i were no longer subject to the despised Internal Revenue Service and its cumbersome gigantic maze of laws that contain enough holes for the wealthy class to supply a doughnut factory for eternity! Looking at the broadest picture, a liberated Hawai'i can deny to the U.S., or other countries bent on imperial domination, the use of its territory as a base of support for the many direct and indirect wars against people who seek independence from assorted tyrants.

An independent Hawai'i can likewise give direct moral and material aid to those people. Hawai'i can show the spirit of aloha by granting at least temporary refugee status to persecuted people the world over, far from the source of their torment, while denying refuge to those who can credibly be charged with war crimes. What an example that would set for other countries! A precedent for such a concept exists in Hawai'i already. In ancient Hawai'i a site existed called the City of Refuge, where those being sought by the authorities would be safe once they could find their way there. It was *kapu* (taboo) to harm anyone there. Imagine inviting desperate political activists fleeing tyrannies around the world knowing there was a safe place to be, like a child finding safety at home with parents after being chased by the school bully.

No one would be forcibly returned to a country where he or she would be afraid for his or her life or of being tortured. Such a model could be replicated elsewhere many times over. What an alternative to being governed by a class of people who have consistently provided military, diplomatic, and economic support to tyrants whose slavish devotion to corporate interests is matched only by the savage repression of people from their own nation! These people desire only what the signers of the Declaration sought: liberty, the pursuit of happiness, and a real say in how they are governed.

What else becomes possible with independence? Control over immigration is a major matter. Right now the population of Hawai'i is somewhere between one and one and a half million. Then there are some six million annual tourists. These numbers put a terrific strain on the infrastructure of Hawai'i, including the water supply, available streets for travel (currently two-hour crawl-pace traffic twice a day is the norm for the 6-lane H-1 Freeway), and park systems. Currently, there is no legal barrier to another 5 million Americans moving to Hawai'i. A true government of Hawai'i could come up with a reasonable non-racial quota system.

Control over its own foreign policy would be another major advantage, *making alliances in Hawai'i's interest,* not those of the U.S. Visualize a political and economic alliance of dozens of small nations working together for their common interests. Such attempts have been tried before, with varying success. Bolder initiatives are needed.

Another important resource, of course, is water. Although Hawai'i is surrounded by thousands of miles of ocean water, fresh water is limited to the amount that falls from the sky and stored in natural lava tubes, unless a serious effort is made with desalinization. Already, drought conditions have led to frequent voluntary restrictions and occasionally mandatory restrictions on residents. However, to the best knowledge of this writer, hotel guests have never had to limit themselves! But water supplies for local farmers come into conflict with water for resort golf courses, with the latter generally getting the preferred position.

Citizenship would be determined by Hawai'i Kingdom law, as modified by a newly elected legislative assembly from strictly within Hawai'i's borders, with rational and objective criteria such as length of time living in Hawai'i, grasp of its history and culture, and allegiance to the renovated government. It would be prudent to examine the practices of a number of countries before making a final determination on what constitutes Hawaiian citizenship.

Land use is crucial. "Highest and best use" would no longer be resort development but high quality organic agriculture and aquaculture, not only to feed Hawai'i's citizens relatively self-sufficiently, but to do its part to feed the world, with informed and democratic decision-making with regard to critically important issues like use of genetically modified organisms, pesticide and herbicide use, and irradiation. A good motto to follow is "trust Mother Nature." Need can finally replace greed as the key economic criterion for use of resources. Relative self-sufficiency should be a long term goal. In this context, a comprehensive review of all Hawaiian land claims, both individual and collective, should be undertaken as one of the highest of priorities, with huge input from Hawaiians themselves. It must be recognized that aboriginal Hawaiians have special rights of seniority to land and water, which no one else there has. This valid claim does not refer to a class of citizenship, however.

Seniority is a well established method of adjusting relative position in society. Those at the front of the line get served first. This seems to be universally understood, even if bullies violate this unspoken rule. Similarly, where labor unions have jurisdiction, workers who have been at a job the longest get the most benefits. There is no question that Hawaiians have the longest seniority in Hawai'i. In a just society, they get served first! This should be regarded as a moral issue, rather than a legal one, in order to avoid a dual class of citizenship. By so doing, it will be possible to reverse the existing well-documented trends in which Hawaiians have disproportionate numbers in prison, on welfare, and with disabilities from chronic diseases, and so on. However, how this moral claim can be implemented justly without evolving different classes of citizenship must be left to those who form a reconstituted government.

It will be possible also to devise a system whereby the bulk of the profits, if not all, from the hotel industry remain in Hawai'i, and are not sent out to New York, Chicago, Toronto, Tokyo, London, Seoul, and Taipei. If done well, it may be possible to generate enough revenue to void all taxation, save maybe income tax at the highest levels. Such a plan would no doubt take decades to evolve, however, but is possible.

How do we get there from here? The obvious first place to start is education. Sovereignty needs to become a major theme of every possible newspaper and magazine in Hawai'i and about Hawai'i. Of course, this immediately brings the sovereignty movement into direct conflict with the current owners of these media, as well as television. We have seen in the U.S. and in other countries how the owners of the mass media can warp the political life of a country to the far political right, consistent with their class interest of maintaining control over the resources of a country and even the thinking of its citizens. The media are not neutral. Accordingly, it is essential for sovereignty supporters to either develop their own mass media or to find a way to "liberate" existing media from corporate control.

Sovereignty ought also to be a universal topic for discussion throughout the education system in Hawai'i. To implement such a curriculum is another aspect of liberation. The number of books and videos on the subject needs to be multiplied, along with competent speakers on the matter. Hawaiian event holidays need to be popularized, so that ever-increasing numbers know and appreciate major events in Hawaiian history.

There is no reason why candidates for office should not be grilled in a confrontational way on their knowledge and stands regarding Hawaiian history and sovereignty. We need to create a climate of opinion that makes it impossible for such candidates to win, if they take the perspective "This is a settled matter; Hawai'i is part of the United States." Visualize unions going beyond the usual concerns of wages, working conditions, and pensions (all necessary, of course) and taking up the matter of sovereignty! Diplomatic and legal channels need to be pursued, adding on to the existing efforts already commenced. People are familiar with the U.S. occupation of Iraq. They need to know that Hawai'i has been occupied for over one hundred years, albeit without a "shock and awe" military campaign. The example of Lithuania provides a concrete model, from which lessons can be learned and applied in the context of Hawai'i.

People will begin to take sovereignty more seriously when the liberation contingent actually begins to govern in small ways. This can be done by building an economic base of pro-sovereignty cooperatives that employ people, providing goods and services that people actually need, not producing plastic trinkets and fad items aggressively promoted to make a fast buck. As jobs currently are being exported overseas, people will be increasingly receptive to new possibilities. Combining imagination with common sense and financial resource pooling, great things can be accomplished. In particular, activists should concentrate on doing what the present government does poorly, such as finding creative ways to adjudicate civil disputes rather than lawsuits that are cumbersome, time-consuming, expensive and often technical. Hawai'i has a long and rich tradition of mediation. Why not make this the preferred manner in which to deal with disputes?

It would be a good idea to make personal contacts among the existing governmental structure and unions so that people so employed will be favorably conditioned toward a smooth transition when the time is right, avoiding having to "reinvent the wheel" of useful administrative procedures. Of course many will be hostile to the idea of an independent Hawai'i, but certainly it will be worthwhile to find those who are open. These people can help already by providing useful information not accessible to the general public. Sovereignty activists can already begin to develop and implement at a preliminary level a Hawaiian foreign policy, especially with small nations who are at the periphery of global imperialism. Hawai'i can provide moral and material support for those engaged in resistance to U.S. domination and to the puppet regimes it sponsors. Activists can invite those so engaged to have conferences in Hawai'i to promote mutual support.

In the furtherance of such perspectives, activists today need to continue to build on past initiatives by creating among all willing residents *a political party dedicated to the liberation of Hawai'i,* using the existing electoral process to promote and defend the concept, and by way of polls and elections, gauge public support.

Another direction by which organized yet peaceful resistance can take place is the formation of creative alternative institutions and methodologies for accomplishing the essential tasks performed today by corporations, but without their waste, redundancy, and greed. Foremost among these would be cooperatives based on internal democracy and mutual respect for each person's unique capabilities to contribute. For instance, it would not be hard to discover what is needed by people, e.g., affordable housing, legal services, and medical care. The next step would be to find those willing to work at pooling resources not to provide free labor charity, but service at a price that serves both the public and those with such a vision at a livable salary/wage.

The image that comes to mind is that of a river encountering a dam. The river "thinks" "OK, if I cannot go through you, I will go around you at the edges." Political control in Hawai'i is like that dam, which like all dams eventually gives way in time. Meanwhile, let us find creative ways to "go around" the obstacle. The battle is on for the allegiance of the people. Once that encounter has been largely achieved, we are half-way there, at least. There are always, in any population, the advanced thinkers, those who will follow, given good leadership, and the retrograde forces who dig in their heels at any change that threatens the *status quo*. It is a waste of time to try to convert the latter. The best strategy is to achieve their political isolation to the point of irrelevance. It would be useful to study the wide range of tactics employed by the Lithuanians in their 50-year successful struggle for liberation, avoiding the errors made (principally armed struggle against a hugely powerful foe) and adopting what they did successfully, with appropriate adaptations, namely cultivating a worldwide support network along with relentless single-minded focus on the goal.

A useful book, published in 1992, points the way to the possibilities in a Hawaiian society liberated from the dead ideas and methods currently prevailing. While not taking the position of promoting independence of Hawai'i from the United States, it addresses innumerable existing consequences of the prevailing dependence, along with creative and enlightened avenues toward a healthier society. This book, written by the key founder of the Hawai'i Green Party, Prof. Ira Rohter, is called *A Green Hawai'i*, published in Hawai'i by a small publisher called Na Kane O Malo Press.

The sheer documentation is voluminous, and is a testament to the excellence of the scholarly effort. The overall theme of the book is to have a radical decentralization of government and immensely more direct participation in the affairs that affect people's lives. Rohter uses the technique of describing his view of how things *should be* from the perspective of the future as if the changes had already taken place. To get the flavor of the book, consider this passage:

> Early on we realized that citizenship can be learned only by involvement, and not from camping in front of a TV set, watching 30-second campaign commercials, staged hoopla-filled rallies, and pseudo-debates. Hawai'i's citizens in 2010 are reared in settings where community and politics meet. Every citizen is a legislator and can make policy in person at the neighborhood

> or *kaioulu* meeting. In any neighborhood, dozens of citizens fill public offices, on a rotating basis, and an even greater number serve as volunteers in myriad other activities. . . . People are willing to take part in decision-making when their actions count. In 2010 our neighborhood or *kaioulu* assemblies have real power. They make policies that directly affect peoples' lives—how to afford a new park, which streets to redesign to be people-friendly, how to pay for international databases and computers at the library, where to put in a new community garden, how to attract light industry, etc. Real control entails spending money, too. Because delegates to higher levels of policy-setting are rooted in and report back to their communities all the time, average citizens also know their discussions and recommendations will count. Participation that is intense, extensive, and lasting only becomes possible when collective decisions govern important facets of people's lives, not just trivial issues. Participation thus has important instrumental effects—people get more of what they want. (2)

With respect to environmental and sustainability issues, Prof. Rohter puts forward this line of reasoning:

> . . .On a global level we were confronted by the depletion of the atmospheric ozone layer, the greenhouse effect, polluted and disappearing water supplies, declining rain forests, overflowing waste water disposal facilities, soil erosion and desertification, destruction of forests by acid rain, and other items in a depressing litany. We began to realize that planning must re-orient itself away from society's one-sided emphasis on growth. Since Adam Smith's days, Western economies have been based on maximization and expansion rather than sufficiency and balance; the monetary

economy has ruled at the expense of the Earth's environment.

We asserted our political control and reminded everyone that an 'economy' was a human construct, a set of values and social arrangements subject not to inexorable natural laws, such as found in physics and chemistry, but to *political choices.* Thus we devised an economic scenario that gave top priority to conservation of energy and the environment, rather than to encouraging 'more and more production' with all its attendant ills. (3)

The late Prof. Rohter visualized very well many specific alternative political and economic structures to further this goal. In the view of this author, also a founding member of the Hawai'i Greens, the excellent ideas for the future it proposes (projected in 1992 to the year 2010) provide sound guidelines *once the stranglehold of U.S. domination has been broken.* Until the vice-like grip of imperial control is cracked, however, I see little chance of these marvelously creative innovations being implemented.

It must be pointed out that the "state" government of Hawai'i is a wholly owned subsidiary of the government of the United States, and any attempts to "reform" that government are doomed to failure with regard to the ultimate liberation of Hawai'i. This is not to say that there are not presently some very capable and honorable people within that government, including the legislature, some of whom are personally known to this author. These are men and women of high moral-political character who try their best to do what is right under the very confining rules implemented by the imposition of the imperial power fused together with the local corporate elite. Efforts must be made to encourage such people of honor to strive for liberation with the people and to be willing to make that decisive break when the time is right.

Among the forms of resistance to imperial domination to be considered is the well-respected tactic of passive resistance. With modest success, some Hawaiian activists have refused to acknowledge the jurisdiction of the prevailing court system over them, as Native Hawaiians who have never given their consent since the 1893 overthrow. Generally, the U.S. court system will not take this issue on, but merely brushes it aside by dismissing such challenges.

Certainly, one of the major objectives for the liberation movement must be effective control of some major media, including television, currently monopolized by corporate interests in service to U.S. imperialism. Such an assertion by no means denigrates the sincere efforts of some Hawai'i reporters and commentators who have the interests of the people at heart. But, like the legislature, the political context under which they must operate is that of the dominant social-political order, namely that of the U.S. Empire.

Renowned navigator of the *Hokule'a* long-distance voyaging canoe Nainoa Thompson has spoken of his mentor, Mau Piailug's, advice to visualize the object of the voyage clearly in his mind, and *allow that vision to guide the voyage.* This is exactly the value of Rohter's book. It helps those engaged on the voyage of the liberation of Hawai'i to see more clearly where to go in terms of a desirable political, social, and economic system that truly reflects the magnificent world-renowned spirit of aloha. It is the goal of this book to have a similar effect.

Appendix A

U.S. President Grover Cleveland's Message to the U.S. Congress of December 18, 1893 concerning The Hawaiian Kingdom investigation.

To the Senate and House of Representatives:
In my recent annual message to the Congress I briefly referred to our relation with Hawaii and expressed the intention of transmitting further information on the subject when additional advises permitted. Though I am not able now to report a definite change in the actual situation, I am convinced that the difficulties lately created both here and in Hawaii and now standing in the way of a solution through Executive action of the problem presented, render it proper, and expedient, that the matter should be referred to the broader authority and discretion of Congress, with a full explanation of the endeavor thus far made to deal with the emergency and a statement of the considerations which have governed my action.
I suppose that right and justice should determine the path to be followed in treating this subject. If national honesty is to be disregarded and a desire for territorial extension, or dissatisfaction with a form of government not our own, ought to regulate our conduct, I have entirely misapprehended the mission and character of our Government and the behavior which the conscience of our people demands of their public servants. When the present Administration entered upon its duties the Senate had under consideration a treaty providing for the annexation of the Hawaiian Islands to the territory of the United States. Surely under our Constitution and laws the enlargement of our limits is a manifestation of the highest attribute of sovereignty, and if entered upon as an Executive act, all things relating to the transaction should be clear and free from suspicion. Additional importance attached to this particular treaty of annexation, because it contemplated a departure from unbroken American tradition in providing for the addition to our territory of islands of the sea more than two

thousand miles removed from our nearest coast.

These considerations might not of themselves call for interference with the completion of a treaty entered upon by a previous Administration. But it appeared from the documents accompanying the treaty when submitted to the Senate, that the ownership of Hawaii was tendered to us by a provisional government set up to succeed the constitutional ruler of the islands, who had been dethroned, and it did not appear that such provisional government had the sanction of either popular revolution or suffrage. Two other remarkable features of the transaction naturally attracted attention. One was the extraordinary haste—not to say precipitancy—characterizing all the transactions connected with the treaty. It appeared that a so-called Committee of Safety, ostensibly the source of the revolt against the constitutional Government of Hawaii, was organized on Saturday, the 14th day of January; that on Monday, the 16th, the United States forces were landed at Honolulu from a naval vessel lying in its harbor; that on the 17th the scheme of a provisional government was perfected, and a proclamation naming its officers was on the same day prepared and read at the Government building; that immediately thereupon the United States Minister recognized the provisional government thus created; that two days afterwards, on the 19th day of January, commissioners representing such government sailed for this country in a steamer especially chartered for the occasion, arriving in San Francisco on the 28th day of January, and in Washington on the 3rd day of February; that on the next day they had their first interview with the Secretary of State, and another on the 11th, when the treaty of annexation was practically agreed upon, and that on the 14th it was formally concluded and on the 15th transmitted to the Senate. Thus between the initiation of the scheme for a provisional government in Hawaii on the 14th day of January and the submission to the Senate of the interval was thirty-two days, fifteen of which were spent by the Hawaiian Commissioners in their journey to Washington.

In the next place, upon the face of the papers submitted with the treaty, it clearly appeared that there was open and undetermined an issue of fact of the most vital importance. The message of the President accompanying the treaty declared that "the overthrow of the monarchy was not in any way promoted by this Government," and in a letter to the President from the Secretary of State, also submitted to the Senate with the treaty, the following passage occurs: "At the time the provisional government took possession of the Government buildings no troops or officers of the United States were present or took any part whatever in the proceedings. No public recognition was accorded to the provisional government by the United States Minister until after the Queen's abdication and when they were in effective possession of the Government buildings, the archives, the treasury, the barracks, the police station, and all the potential machinery of the Government." But a protest also accompanied said treaty, signed by the Queen and her ministers at the time she made way for the provisional government, which explicitly stated that she yielded to the superior force of the United States, whose Minister had caused United States troops to be landed at Honolulu and declared that he would support such provisional government. The truth or falsity of this protest was surely of the first importance. If true, nothing but the concealment of its truth could induce our Government to negotiate with the semblance of a government thus created, nor could a treaty resulting from the acts stated in the protest have been knowingly deemed worthy of consideration by the Senate. Yet the truth or falsity of the protest had not been investigated.

I conceived it to be my duty therefore to withdraw the treaty from the Senate for examination, and meanwhile to cause an accurate, full, and impartial investigation to be made of the facts attending the subversion of the constitutional Government of Hawaii, and the installment in its place of the provisional government. I selected for the work of investigation the Hon. James H. Blount, of Georgia, whose service of eighteen years as a member of the House of Representatives, and whose experience as chairman of the Committee of Foreign Affairs in that body, and his consequent familiarity with international topics, joined with his character and honorable reputation, seemed to render him peculiarly fitted for the duties entrusted to him. His report detailing his action under the instructions given to him and the conclusions derived from his investigation accompany this message.

These conclusions do not rest for their acceptance entirely upon Mr. Blount's honesty and ability as a man, nor upon his acumen and impartiality as an investigator. They are accompanied by the evidence upon which they are based, which evidence is also herewith transmitted, and from which it seems to me no other deductions could possibly be reached than those arrived at by the Commissioner.

The report with its accompanying proofs, and such other evidence as is now before the Congress or is herewith submitted, justifies in my opinion the statement that when the President was led to submit the treaty to the Senate with the declaration that "the overthrow of the monarchy was not in any way promoted by this Government," and when the Senate was induced to receive and discuss it on that basis, both President and Senate were misled.

The attempt will not be made in this communication to touch upon all the facts which throw light upon the progress and consummation of this scheme of annexation. A very brief and imperfect reference to the facts and evidence at hand will exhibit its character and the incidents in which it had its birth.

It is unnecessary to set forth the reasons which in January, 1893, led a considerable proportion of American and other foreign merchants and traders residing at Honolulu to favor the annexation of Hawaii to the United States. It is sufficient to note the fact and to observe that the project was one which was zealously promoted by the Minister representing the United States in that country. He evidently had an ardent desire that it should become a fact accomplished by his agency and during his ministry, and was not inconveniently scrupulous as to the means employed to that end. On the 19th day of November, 1892, nearly two months before the first overt act tending towards the subversion of the Hawaiian Government and the attempted transfer of Hawaiian territory to the United States, he addressed a long letter to the Secretary of State in which the case for annexation was elaborately argued, on moral, political, and economical grounds. He refers to the loss to the Hawaiian sugar interests from the operation of the McKinley bill, and the tendency to still further depreciation of sugar property unless some positive measure of relief is granted. He strongly inveighs against the existing Hawaiian Government and emphatically declares for annexation. He says: "In truth the monarchy here is an absurd anachronism. It has nothing on which it logically or legitimately stands. The feudal basis on which it once stood no longer existing, the monarchy now is only an impediment to good government—an obstruction to the prosperity and progress of the islands."

He further says: "As a crown colony of Great Britain or a Territory of the United States the government modifications could be made readily and good administration of the law secured. Destiny and the vast future interests of the United States in the Pacific clearly indicate who at no distant day must be responsible for the government of these islands. Under a territorial government they could be as easily governed as any of the existing Territories of the United States." * * * "Hawaii has reached the parting of the ways. She must now take the road which leads to Asia, or the other which outlets her in America, gives her an American civilization, and binds her to the care of American destiny." He also declares: "One of two courses seems to me absolutely necessary to be followed, either bold and vigorous measures for annexation or a 'customs union,' an ocean cable from the California coast to Honolulu, Pearl Harbor perpetually ceded to the United States, with an implied but not expressly stipulated American protectorate over the islands. I believe the former to be the better, that which will prove much the more advantageous to the islands, and the cheapest and least embarrassing in the end to the United States. If it was wise for the United States through Secretary Marcy thirty-eight years ago to offer to expend $100,000 to secure a treaty of annexation, it certainly can not be chimerical or unwise to expend $100,000 to secure annexation in the near future. Today the United States has five times the wealth she possessed in 1854, and the reasons now existing for annexation are much stronger than they were then. I can not refrain from expressing the opinion with emphasis that the golden hour is near at hand."

These declarations certainly show a disposition and condition of mind, which may be usefully recalled when interpreting the significance of the Minister's conceded acts or when considering the probabilities of such conduct on his part as may not be admitted.

In this view it seems proper to also quote from a letter written by the Minister to the Secretary of State on the 8th day of March, 1892, nearly a year prior to the first step taken toward annexation. After stating the possibility that the existing Government of Hawaii might be over turned by an orderly and peaceful revolution, Minister Stevens writes as follows: "Ordinarily in like circumstances, the rule seems to be to limit the landing and movement of United States forces in foreign waters and dominion exclusively to the protection of the United States legation and of the lives and property of American citizens. But as the relations of the United States to Hawaii are exceptional, and in former years the United States officials here took somewhat exceptional action in circumstances of disorder, I desire to know how far the present Minister and naval commander may deviate from established international rules and precedent in the contingencies indicated in the first part of this dispatch."

To a minister of this temper full of zeal for annexation there seemed to arise in January, 1893, the precise opportunity for which he was watchfully waiting-an opportunity which by timely "deviation from established international rules and precedents" might be improved to successfully accomplish the great object in view; and we are quite prepared for the exultant enthusiasm with which in a letter to the State Department dated February 1, 1893, he declares: "The Hawaiian pear is now fully ripe and this is the golden hour for the United States to pluck it."

As a further illustration of the activity of this diplomatic representative, attention is called to the fact that on the day the above letter was written apparently unable longer to restrain his ardor, he issued a proclamation whereby "in the name of the United States" he assumed the protection of the Hawaiian Islands and declared that said action was "taken pending and subject to negotiations at Washington." Of course this assumption of a protectorate was promptly disavowed by our Government, but the American flag remained over the Government building at Honolulu and the forces remained on guard until April, and after Mr. Blount's arrival on the scene, when both were removed.

A brief statement of the occurrences that led to the subversion of the constitutional Government of Hawaii in the interest of annexation to the United States will exhibit the true complexion of that transaction. On Saturday, January 14, 1893, the Queen of Hawaii, who had been contemplating the proclamation of a new constitution, had, in deference to the wishes and remonstrances of her cabinet, renounced the project for the present at least. Taking this relinquished purpose as a basis of action, citizens of Honolulu numbering from fifty to one hundred, mostly resident aliens, met in a private office and selected a so-called Committee of Safety, composed of thirteen persons, seven of whom were foreign subjects, and consisted of five Americans, one Englishman, and one German. This committee, though its designs were not revealed, had in view nothing less than annexation to the United States, and between Saturday, the 14th, and the following Monday, the 16th of January—though exactly what action was taken may not be clearly disclosed—they were certainly in communication with the United States Minister. On Monday morning the Queen and her cabinet made a public proclamation, with a notice which was specially served upon the representatives of all foreign governments, that any changes in the constitution would be sought only in the methods provided by that instrument. Nevertheless, at the call and under the auspices of the Committee of Safety, a mass meeting of citizens was held on that day to protest against the Queen's alleged illegal and unlawful proceedings and purposes. Even at this meeting the Committee of Safety continued to disguise their real purpose and contented themselves with procuring the passage of a resolution denouncing the Queen and empowering the committee to devise ways and means "to secure the permanent maintenance of law and order and the protection of life, liberty, and property in Hawaii." This meeting adjourned between three and four o'clock in the afternoon. On the same day, and immediately after such adjournment, the committee, unwilling to take further steps without the cooperation of the United States Minister, addressed him a note representing that the public safety was menaced and that lives and property were in danger, and concluded as follows: "We are unable to protect ourselves without aid, and therefore pray for the protection of the United States forces." Whatever may be thought of the other contents of this note, the absolute truth of this latter statement is incontestable. When the note was written and delivered, the committee, so far as it appears, had neither a man nor a gun at their command, and after its delivery they became so panic-stricken at their position that they sent some of their number to interview the Minister and request him not to land the United States forces till the next morning. But he replied that the troops had been ordered, and whether the committee were ready or not the landing should take place. And so it happened that on the 16th day of January, 1893, between four and five o'clock in the afternoon, a detachment of marines from the United States steamer Boston, with two pieces of artillery, landed at Honolulu. The men, upwards of 160 in all, were supplied with double cartridge belts filled with ammunition and with haversacks and canteens, and were accompanied by a hospital corps with stretchers and medical supplies. This military demonstration upon the soil of Honolulu was of itself an act of war, unless made either with the consent of the Government of Hawaii or for the bona fide purpose of protecting the imperiled lives and property of citizens of the United States. But there is no pretense of any such consent on the part of the Government of the Queen, which at that time was undisputed and was both the de facto and the de jure government. In point of fact the existing government instead of requesting the presence of an armed force protested against it. There is as little basis for the pretense that such forces were landed for the security of American life and property. If so, they would have been stationed in the vicinity of such property and so as to protect it, instead of at a distance and so as to command the Hawaiian Government building and palace. Admiral Skerrett, the officer in command of our naval force on the Pacific station, has frankly stated that in his opinion the location of the troops was inadvisable if they were landed for the protection of American citizens whose residences and places of business, as well as the legation and consulate, were in a distant part of the city, but the location selected was a wise one if the forces were landed for the purpose of supporting the provisional government. If any peril to life and property calling for any such martial array had existed, Great Britain and other foreign powers interested would not have been behind the United States in activity to protect their citizens. But they made no sign in that direction. When these armed men were landed, the city of Honolulu was in its customary orderly and peaceful condition. There was no symptom of riot or disturbance in any quarter. Men, women, and children were about the streets as usual, and nothing varied the ordinary routine or disturbed the ordinary tranquility, except the landing of the Boston's marines and their march through the town to the quarters assigned them. Indeed, the fact that after having called for the landing of the United States forces on the plea of danger to life and property the Committee of Safety themselves requested the Minister to postpone action, exposed the untruthfulness of their representations of present peril to life and property. The peril they saw was an anticipation growing out of guilty intentions on their part and something which, though not then existing, they knew would certainly follow their attempt to overthrow the Government of the Queen without the aid of the United States forces. Thus it appears that Hawaii was taken possession of by the United States forces without the consent or wish of the government of the islands, or of anybody else so far as shown, except the United States Minister.

Therefore the military occupation of Honolulu by the United States on the day mentioned was wholly without justification, either as an occupation by consent or as an occupation necessitated by dangers threatening American life and property. It must be accounted for in some other way and on some other ground, and its real motive and purpose are neither obscure nor far to seek.

The United States forces being now on the scene and favorably stationed, the committee proceeded to carry out their original scheme. They met the next morning, Tuesday, the 17th, perfected the plan of temporary government, and fixed upon its principal officers, ten of whom were drawn from the thirteen members of the Committee of Safety. Between one and two o'clock, by squads and by different routes to avoid notice, and having first taken the precaution of ascertaining whether there was any one there to oppose them, they proceeded to the Government building almost entirely without auditors. It is said that before the reading was finished quite a concourse of persons, variously estimated at from 50 to 100, some armed and some unarmed, gathered about the committee to give them aid and confidence. This statement is not important, since the one controlling factor in the whole affair was unquestionably the United States marines, who, drawn up under arms and with artillery in readiness only seventy-six yards distant, dominated the situation.

The provisional government thus proclaimed was by the terms of the proclamation "to exist until terms of union with the United States had been negotiated and agreed upon." The United States Minister, pursuant to prior agreement, recognized this government within an hour after the reading of the proclamation, and before five o'clock, in answer to any inquiry on behalf of the Queen and her cabinet, announced that he had done so.

When our Minister recognized the provisional government the only basis upon which it rested was the fact that the Committee of Safety had in the manner above stated declared it to exist. It was neither a government de facto nor de jure. That it was not in such possession of the Government property and agencies as entitled it to recognition is conclusively proved by a note found in the files of the Legation at Honolulu, addressed by the declared head of the provisional government to Minister Stevens, dated January 17, 1893, in which he acknowledges with expressions of appreciation the Minister's recognition of the provisional government, and states that it is not yet in the possession of the station house (the place where a large number of the Queen's troops were quartered), though the same had been demanded of the Queen's officers in charge. Nevertheless, this wrongful recognition by our Minister placed the Government of the Queen in a position of most perilous perplexity. On the one hand she had possession of the palace, of the barracks, and of the police station, and had at her command at least five hundred fully armed men and several pieces of artillery.indeed, the whole military force of her kingdom was on her side and at her disposal, while the Committee of Safety, by actual search, had discovered that there were but very few arms in Honolulu that were not in the service of the Government. In this state of things if the Queen could have dealt with the insurgents alone her course would have been plain and the result unmistakable. But the United States had allied itself with her enemies, had recognized them as the true Government of Hawaii, and had put her and her adherents in the position of opposition against lawful authority. She knew that she could not withstand the power of the United States, but she believed that she might safely trust to its justice. Accordingly, some hours after the recognition of the provisional government by the United States Minister, the palace, the barracks, and the police station, with all the military resources of the country, were delivered up by the Queen upon the representation made to her that her cause would thereafter be reviewed at Washington, and while protesting that she surrendered to the superior force of the United States, whose Minister had caused United States troops to be landed at Honolulu and declared that he would support the provisional government, and that she yielded her authority to prevent collision of armed forces and loss of life and only until such time as the United States, upon the facts being presented to it, should undo the action of its representative and reinstate her in the authority she claimed as the constitutional sovereign of the Hawaiian Islands.

This protest was delivered to the chief of the provisional government, who endorsed thereon his acknowledgment of its receipt. The terms of the protest were read without dissent by those assuming to constitute the provisional government, who were certainly charged with the knowledge that the Queen instead of finally abandoning her power had appealed to the justice of the United States for reinstatement in her authority; and yet the provisional government with this unanswered protest in its hand hastened to negotiate with the United States for the permanent banishment of the Queen from power and for the sale of her kingdom.

Our country was in danger of occupying the position of having actually set up a temporary government on foreign soil for the purpose of acquiring through that agency territory which we had wrongfully put in its possession. The control of both sides of a bargain acquired in such a manner is called by a familiar and unpleasant name when found in private transactions. We are not without a precedent showing how scrupulously we avoided such accusations in former days. After the people of Texas had declared their independence of Mexico they resolved that on the acknowledgment of their independence by the United States they would seek admission into the Union. Several months after the battle of San Jacinto, by which Texan independence was practically assured and established, President Jackson declined to recognize it, alleging as one of his reasons that in the circumstances it became us "to beware of a too early movement, as it might subject us, however unjustly, to the imputation of seeking to establish the claim of our neighbors to a territory with a view to its subsequent acquisition by ourselves." This is in marked contrast with the hasty recognition of a government openly and concededly set up for the purpose of tendering to us territorial annexation.

I believe that a candid and thorough examination of the facts will force the conviction that the provisional government owes its existence to an armed invasion by the United States. Fair-minded people with the evidence before them will hardly claim that the Hawaiian Government was overthrown by the people of the islands or that the provisional government had ever existed with their consent. I do not understand that any member of this government claims that the people would uphold it by their suffrages if they were allowed to vote on the question. While naturally sympathizing with every effort to establish a republican form of government, it has been the settled policy of the United States to concede to people of foreign countries the same freedom and independence in the management of their domestic affairs that we have always claimed for ourselves; and it has been our practice to recognize revolutionary governments as soon as it became apparent that they were supported by the people. For illustration of this rule I need only to refer to the revolution in Brazil in 1889, when our Minister was instructed to recognize the Republic "so soon as a majority of the people of Brazil should have signified their assent to its establishment and maintenance"; to the revolution in Chile in 1891,when our Minister was directed to recognize the new government "if it was accepted by the people"; and to the revolution in Venezuela in 1892, when our recognition was accorded on condition that the new government was "fully established, in possession of the power of the nation, and accepted by the people."

As I apprehend the situation, we are brought face to face with the following conditions:

The lawful Government of Hawaii was overthrown without the drawing of a sword or the firing of a shot by a process every step of which, it may be safely asserted, is directly traceable to and dependent for its success upon the agency of the United States acting through its diplomatic and naval representatives. But for the notorious predilections of the United States Minister for annexation, the Committee of Safety, which should be called the Committee of Annexation, would never have existed.

But for the landing of the United States forces upon false pretexts respecting the danger to life and property the committee would never have exposed themselves to the pains and penalties of treason by undertaking the subversion of the Queen's Government.

But for the presence of the United States forces in the immediate vicinity and in position to afford all needed protection and support the committee would not have proclaimed the provisional government from the steps of the Government building.

And finally, but for the lawless occupation of Honolulu under false pretexts by the United States forces, and but for Minister Stevens' recognition of the provisional government when the United States forces were its sole support and constituted its only military strength, the Queen and her Government would never have yielded to the provisional government, even for a time and for the sole purpose of submitting her case to the enlightened justice of the United States.

Believing, therefore, that the United States could not, under the circumstances disclosed, annex the islands without justly incurring the imputation of acquiring them by unjustifiable methods, I shall not again submit the treaty of annexation to the Senate for its consideration, and in the instructions to Minister Willis, a copy of which accompanies this message, I have directed him to so inform the provisional government.

But in the present instance our duty does not, in my opinion, end with refusing to consummate this questionable transaction. It has been the boast of our government that it seeks to do justice in all things without regard to the strength or weakness of those with whom it deals. I mistake the American people if they favor the odious doctrine that there is no such thing as international morality, that there is one law for a strong nation and another for a weak one, and that even by indirection a strong power may with impunity despoil a weak one of its territory.

By an act of war, committed with the participation of a diplomatic representative of the United States and without authority of Congress, the Government of a feeble but friendly and confiding people has been overthrown. A substantial wrong has thus been done which a due regard for our national character as well as the rights of the injured people requires we should endeavor to repair. The provisional government has not assumed a republican or other constitutional form, but has remained a mere executive council or oligarchy, set up without the assent of the people. It has not sought to find a permanent basis of popular support and has given no evidence of an intention to do so. Indeed, the representatives of that government assert that the people of Hawaii are unfit for popular government and frankly avow that they can be best ruled by arbitrary or despotic power.

The law of nations is founded upon reason and justice, and

the rules of conduct governing individual relations between citizens or subjects of a civilized state are equally applicable as between enlightened nations. The considerations that international law is without a court for its enforcement, and that obedience to its commands practically depends upon good faith, instead of upon the mandate of a superior tribunal, only give additional sanction to the law itself and brand any deliberate infraction of it not merely as a wrong but as a disgrace. A man of true honor protects the unwritten word which binds his conscience more scrupulously, if possible, than he does the bond a breach of which subjects him to legal liabilities; and the United States in aiming to maintain itself as one of the most enlightened of nations would do its citizens gross injustice if it applied to its international relations any other than a high standard of honor and morality. On that ground the United States can not properly be put in the position of countenancing a wrong after its commission any more than in that of consenting to it in advance. On that ground it can not allow itself to refuse to redress an injury inflicted through an abuse of power by officers clothed with its authority and wearing its uniform; and on the same ground, if a feeble but friendly state is in danger of being robbed of its independence and its sovereignty by a misuse of the name and power of the United States, the United States can not fail to vindicate its honor and its sense of justice by an earnest effort to make all possible reparation.

These principles apply to the present case with irresistible force when the special conditions of the Queen's surrender of her sovereignty are recalled. She surrendered not to the provisional government, but to the United States. She surrendered not absolutely and permanently, but temporarily and conditionally until such time as the facts could be considered by the United States. Furthermore, the provisional government acquiesced in her surrender in that manner and on those terms, not only by tacit consent, but through the positive acts of some members of that government who urged her peaceable submission, not merely to avoid bloodshed, but because she could place implicit reliance upon the justice of the United States, and that the whole subject would be finally considered at Washington.

I have not, however, overlooked an incident of this unfortunate affair which remains to be mentioned. The members of the provisional government and their supporters, though not entitled to extreme sympathy, have been led to their present predicament of revolt against the Government of the Queen by the indefensible encouragement and assistance of our diplomatic representative. This fact may entitle them to claim that in our effort to rectify the wrong committed some regard should be had for their safety. This sentiment is strongly seconded by my anxiety to do nothing which would invite either harsh retaliation on the part of the Queen or violence and bloodshed in any quarter. In the belief that the Queen, as well as her enemies, would be willing to adopt such a course as would meet these conditions, and in view of the fact that both the Queen and the provisional government had at one time apparently acquiesced in a reference of the entire case to the United States Government, and considering the further fact that in any event the provisional government by its own declared limitation was only "to exist until terms of union with the United States of America have been negotiated and agreed upon," I hoped that after the assurance to the members of that government that such union could not be consummated I might compass a peaceful adjustment of the difficulty.

Actuated by these desires and purposes, and not unmindful of the inherent perplexities of the situation nor of the limitations upon my power, I instructed Minister Willis to advise the Queen and her supporters of my desire to aid in the restoration of the status existing before the lawless landing of the United States forces at Honolulu on the 16th of January last, if such restoration could be effected upon terms providing for clemency as well as justice to all parties concerned. The conditions suggested, as the instructions show, contemplate a general amnesty to those concerned in setting up the provisional government and a recognition of all its bona fide acts and obligations. In short, they require that the past should be buried, and that the restored Government should reassume its authority as if its continuity had not been interrupted. These conditions have not proved acceptable to the Queen, and though she has been informed that they will be insisted upon, and that, unless acceded to, the efforts of the President to aid in the restoration of her Government will cease, I have not thus far learned that she is willing to yield them her acquiescence. The check which my plans have thus encountered has prevented their presentation to the members of the provisional government, while unfortunate public misrepresentations of the situation and exaggerated statements of the sentiments of our people have obviously injured the prospects of successful Executive mediation.

I therefore submit this communication with its accompanying exhibits, embracing Mr. Blount's report, the evidence and statements taken by him at Honolulu, the instructions given to both Mr. Blount and Minister Willis, and correspondence connected with the affair in hand.

In commending this subject to the extended powers and wide discretion of the Congress, I desire to add the assurance that I shall be much gratified to cooperate in any legislative plan which may be devised for the solution of the problem before us which is consistent with American honor, integrity, and morality.

Grover Cleveland Executive Mansion, Washington, December 18, 1893.

The Executive Documents of the United States House of Representatives, 53rd Congress, 1894-95, Appendix II, Foreign Relations, 1894, Affairs in Hawai'i, volumes 1 and 2.

Appendix B

1993 U.S. Apology Resolution

To acknowledge the 100th anniversary of the January 17, 1893 overthrow of the Kingdom of Hawaii, and to offer an apology to Native Hawaiians on behalf of the United States for the overthrow of the Kingdom of Hawaii.

Whereas, prior to the arrival of the first Europeans in 1778, the Native Hawaiian people lived in a highly organized, self-sufficient, subsistent social system based on communal land tenure with a sophisticated language, culture, and religion;

Whereas, a unified monarchical government of the Hawaiian Islands was established in 1810 under Kamehameha I, the first King of Hawaii;

Whereas, from 1826 until 1893, the United States recognized the independence of the Kingdom of Hawaii, extended full and complete diplomatic recognition to the Hawaiian Government, and entered into treaties and conventions with the Hawaiian monarchs to govern commerce and navigation in 1826, 1842, 1849, 1875, and 1887;

Whereas, the Congregational Church (now known as the United Church of Christ), through its American Board of Commissioners for Foreign Missions, sponsored and sent more than 100 missionaries to the Kingdom of Hawaii between 1820 and 1850;

Whereas, on January 14, 1893, John L. Stevens (hereafter referred to in this Resolution as the "United States Minister"), the United States Minister assigned to the sovereign and independent Kingdom of Hawaii conspired with a small group of non-Hawaiian residents of the Kingdom of Hawaii, including citizens of the United States, to overthrow the indigenous and lawful Government of Hawaii;

Whereas, in pursuance of the conspiracy to overthrow the Government of Hawaii, the United States Minister and the naval representatives of the United States caused armed naval forces of the United States to invade the sovereign Hawaiian nation on January 16, 1893, and to position themselves near

the Hawaiian Government buildings and the lolani Palace to intimidate Queen Liliuokalani and her Government;
Whereas, on the afternoon of January 17,1893, a Committee of Safety that represented the American and European sugar planters, descendants of missionaries, and financiers deposed the Hawaiian monarchy and proclaimed the establishment of a Provisional Government;
Whereas, the United States Minister thereupon extended diplomatic recognition to the Provisional Government that was formed by the conspirators without the consent of the Native Hawaiian people or the lawful Government of Hawaii and in violation of treaties between the two nations and of international law;
Whereas, soon thereafter, when informed of the risk of bloodshed with resistance, Queen Liliuokalani issued the following statement yielding her authority to the United States Government rather than to the Provisional Government:
"I Liliuokalani, by the Grace of God and under the Constitution of the Hawaiian Kingdom, Queen, do hereby solemnly protest against any and all acts done against myself and the Constitutional Government of the Hawaiian Kingdom by certain persons claiming to have established a Provisional Government of and for this Kingdom.
"That I yield to the superior force of the United States of America whose Minister Plenipotentiary, His Excellency John L. Stevens, has caused United States troops to be landed a Honolulu and declared that he would support the Provisional Government.
"Now to avoid any collision of armed forces, and perhaps the loss of life, I do this under protest and impelled by said force yield my authority until such time as the Government of the United States shall, upon facts being presented to it, undo the action of its representatives and reinstate me in the authority which I claim as the Constitutional Sovereign of the Hawaiian Islands.".
Done at Honolulu this 17th day of January, A.D. 1893.;

Whereas, without the active support and intervention by the United States diplomatic and military representatives, the insurrection against the Government of Queen Liliuokalani would have failed for lack of popular support and insufficient arms;

Whereas, on February 1, 1893, the United States Minister raised the American flag and proclaimed Hawaii to be a protectorate of the United States;

Whereas, the report of a Presidentially established investigation conducted by former Congressman James Blount into the events surrounding the insurrection and overthrow of January 17, 1893, concluded

that the United States diplomatic and military representatives had abused their authority and were responsible for the change in government;

Whereas, as a result of this investigation, the United States Minister to Hawaii was recalled from his diplomatic post and the military commander of the United States armed forces stationed in Hawaii was disciplined and forced to resign his commission;

Whereas, in a message to Congress on December 18, 1893, President Grover Cleveland reported fully and accurately on the illegal acts of the conspirators, described such acts as an "act of war, committed with the participation of a diplomatic representative of the United States and without authority of Congress," and acknowledged that by such acts the government of a peaceful and friendly people was overthrown;

Whereas, President Cleveland further concluded that a "substantial wrong has thus been done which a due regard for our national character as well as the rights of the injured people requires we should endeavor to repair" and called for the restoration of the Hawaiian monarchy;

Whereas, the Provisional Government protested President Cleveland's call for the restoration of the monarchy and continued to hold state power and pursue annexation to the United States;

Whereas, the Provisional Government successfully lobbied the Committee on Foreign Relations of the Senate (hereafter referred to in this Resolution as the "Committee") to conduct a new investigation into the events surrounding the overthrow of the monarchy;
Whereas, the Committee and its chairman, Senator John Morgan, conducted hearings in Washington, D.C., from December 27,1893, through February 26, 1894, in which members of the Provisional Government justified and condoned the actions of the United States Minister and recommended annexation of Hawaii;
Whereas, although the Provisional Government was able to obscure the role of the United States in the illegal overthrow of the Hawaiian monarchy, it was unable to rally the support from two-thirds of the Senate needed to ratify a treaty of annexation;
Whereas, on July 4, 1894, the Provisional Government declared itself to be the Republic of Hawaii;
Whereas, on January 24, 1895, while imprisoned in lolani Palace, Queen Liliuokalani was forced by representatives of the Republic of Hawaii to officially abdicate her throne;
Whereas, in the 1896 United States Presidential election, William McKinley replaced Grover Cleveland;
Whereas, on July 7, 1898, as a consequence of the Spanish-American War, President McKinley signed the Newlands Joint Resolution that provided for the annexation of Hawaii;
Whereas, through the Newlands Resolution, the self-declared Republic of Hawaii ceded sovereignty over the Hawaiian Islands to the United States;
Whereas, the Republic of Hawaii also ceded 1,800,000 acres of crown, government and public lands of the Kingdom of Hawaii, without the consent of or compensation to the Native Hawaiian people of Hawaii or their sovereign government;
Whereas, the Congress, through the Newlands Resolution, ratified the cession, annexed Hawaii as part of the United States, and vested title to the lands in Hawaii in the United States;

Whereas, the Newlands Resolution also specified that treaties existing between Hawaii and foreign nations were to immediately cease and be replaced by United States treaties with such nations;
Whereas, the Newlands Resolution effected the transaction between the Republic of Hawaii and the United States Government;
Whereas, the indigenous Hawaiian people never directly relinquished their claims to their inherent sovereignty as a people or over their national lands to the United States, either through their monarchy or through a plebiscite or referendum;
Whereas, on April 30, 1900, President McKinley signed the Organic Act that provided a government for the territory of Hawaii and defined the political structure and powers of the newly established Territorial Government and its relationship to the United States;
Whereas, on August 21,1959, Hawaii became the 50th State of the United States;
Whereas, the health and well-being of the Native Hawaiian people is intrinsically tied to their deep feelings and attachment to the land;
Whereas, the long-range economic and social changes in Hawaii over the nineteenth and early twentieth centuries have been devastating to the population and to the health and well-being of the Hawaiian people;
Whereas, the Native Hawaiian people are determined to preserve, develop and transmit to future generations their ancestral territory, and their cultural identity in accordance with their own spiritual and traditional beliefs, customs, practices, language, and social institutions;
Whereas, in order to promote racial harmony and cultural understanding, the Legislature of the State of Hawaii has determined that the year 1993, should serve Hawaii as a year of special reflection on the rights and dignities of the Native Hawaiians in the Hawaiian and the American societies;
Whereas, the Eighteenth General Synod of the United Church

of Christ in recognition of the denomination's historical complicity in the illegal overthrow of the Kingdom of Hawaii in 1893 directed the Office of the President of the United Church of Christ to offer a public apology to the Native Hawaiian people and to initiate the process of reconciliation between the United Church of Christ and the Native Hawaiians; and

Whereas, it is proper and timely for the Congress on the occasion of the impending one hundredth anniversary of the event, to acknowledge the historic significance of the illegal overthrow of the Kingdom of Hawaii, to express its deep regret to the Native Hawaiian people, and to support the reconciliation efforts of the State of Hawaii and the United Church of Christ with Native Hawaiians;

Now, therefore, be it

Resolved by the Senate and House of Representatives of the United States of America in Congress assembled,

SECTION 1. ACKNOWLEDGMENT AND APOLOGY.

The Congress

(1) on the occasion of the 100th anniversary of the illegal overthrow of the Kingdom of Hawaii on January 17, 1893, acknowledges the historical significance of this event which resulted in the suppression of the inherent sovereignty of the Native Hawaiian people;

(2) recognizes and commends efforts of reconciliation initiated by the State of Hawaii and the United Church of Christ with Native Hawaiians;

(3) apologizes to Native Hawaiians on behalf of the people of the United States for the overthrow of the Kingdom of Hawaii on January 17, 1893 with the participation of agents and citizens of the United States, and the deprivation of the rights of Native Hawaiians to self-determination;

(4) expresses its commitment to acknowledge the ramifications of the overthrow of the Kingdom of Hawaii, in order to provide a proper foundation for reconciliation between the United States and the Native Hawaiian people; and

(5) urges the President of the United States to also

acknowledge the ramifications of the overthrow of the Kingdom of Hawaii and to support reconciliation efforts between the United States and the Native Hawaiian people.

SEC. 2. DEFINITIONS.

As used in this Joint Resolution, the term "Native Hawaiian" means any individual who is a descendent of the aboriginal people who, prior to 1778, occupied and exercised sovereignty in the area that now constitutes the State of Hawaii.

SEC. 3. DISCLAIMER.

Nothing in this Joint Resolution is intended to serve as a settlement of any claims against the United States.

U.S. Public Law 103-150, 103rd Congress, Joint Resolution to acknowledge the 100th anniversary of the January 17, 1893 overthrow of the Kingdom of Hawai'i, November 3, 1993.

One sovereignty organization, Ke Puni O Hawaii Nei, has put forth a proposal for citizenship criteria, such as all countries have. This author is not claiming that the perspective is universally accepted in Hawai'i, but is suggesting that at least it is at good place to start discussion. Clearly the intent is non racial, in that there is no intent to exclude anyone from citizenship or residence based on ethnicity.

Appendix C

Types of Hawaiian Kingdom Citizenship:
The following are the various types of Citizenship that exist under Hawaiian Kingdom Law. There are five (5) distinct types of citizenship that apply to Hawaiians. "Hawaiian" is a nationality, not just a bloodline of the Native Hawaiian People.
Citizens Born To the Hawaiian Archipelago Are Hawaiian by Birth. Birth Certificate is Evidence of Hawaiian Nationality.

1. The first and primary type of citizenship is that of the natural born "Hawaiian" of native Hawaiian ancestry. These Hawaiians have the greatest interest, being stewards of the aina. These Hawaiians have a vested interest in the aina, as affirmed by the Great Mahele.
2. The second type of "Hawaiian," is one who does not have native Hawaiian blood, but is born in Hawaii.
3. The third type of citizenship is that of one "born abroad" to parents of Hawaiian Citizenship. This individual has the choice of dual citizenship. At the age of consent, this foreign born has choice of citizenship of the nation of birth or that of their Hawaiian parents.
4. The fourth type of citizenship is that of a "naturalized" citizen, who has taken an oath to become a Hawaiian Citizen after first renouncing his or her country of birth citizenship. This is accomplished in a Circuit Court of the Hawaiian Kingdom.

5. The fifth type of citizenship is a dual citizenship. A "denizen" is one who retains foreign citizenship but who is under lawful oath of allegiance to the Hawaiian Kingdom Constitution and Hawaiian Kingdom laws.

The above is submitted for the understanding and awareness of all individuals who may have concerns as to the types of citizenship within the Hawaiian Kingdom and how they are distinguished from one another.

Bibliography

American Friends Service Committee (Hawai'i). FACT SHEET ON U.S. MILITARY IN HAWAI'I—JUNE 23, 2004.

Cleveland, Grover. *Message to the United States Congress.* Washington: December 18, 1893. The Executive Documents of the United States House of Representatives, 53rd Congress, 1894-95, Appendix II, Foreign Relations, 1894, Affairs in Hawai'i, volumes 1 and 2.

Coffman, Tom. *Nation Within: The History of the American Occupation of Hawai'i.* (Revised Edition) Kihei, Hawai'i: Koa Books. 2009.

Gerutis, Albertas, editor. *Lithuania 700 Years.* Translated by Algirdas Budrekis. New York: Manyland Books, Second Revised Edition, 1969.

"The Importance of Annexation to Kanaka Maoli today," in *Self Determination,* Newsletter of the Kanaka Maoli Tribunal Komike. March 1998.

Joint Resolution of United States Congress: *Apology Resolution.* U.S. Public Law 103-150, 103rd Congress, Joint Resolution to acknowledge the 100th anniversary of the January 17, 1893 overthrow of the Kingdom of Hawai'i, November 3, 1993.

Kelly, Anna Keala. *Statement in Opposition to the Akaka Bill,* presented orally to the Akaka Bill Forum at Japanese Chamber of Commerce, Aug. 23, 2005.

Kelly, Marion. E-mailed report to author, 6/26/2004.

Kent, Noel. *Islands Under the Influence.* New York: Monthly Review Press. 1983.

Krikus, Richard J. *Showdown: The Lithuanian Rebellion and the Breakup of the Soviet Empire.* Brassey's Inc. Washington, London, 1997.

Liliuokalani. *Hawaii's Story by Hawaii's Queen.* Honolulu, Hawaii: Mutual Publishing. Fifth Printing, June 1999. (Reprint of original 1898 edition.)

Low, Sam, "Voyages of Awakening" in *Hana Hou!* Vol. 3 number 1 February/March, 2000.

Naylor, Thomas. "The Manifesto."

Paik, Koohan, and Jerry Mander. *The Superferry Chronicles: Hawaii's Uprising Against Militarism, Commercialism, and the Desecration of the Earth.* Kihei, Hawai'i: Koa Books, 2009.

Sai, David Keanu. *Dominion of the Hawaiian Kingdom.* Private Publication. Honolulu, Hawai'i, 2001. This document was prepared for the United Nations' Security Council as an attachment to the Complaint filed by the Hawaiian Kingdom against the United States of America, 5 July 2001.

Sai, David Keanu. PhD. "1893 Cleveland-Lili'uokalani Executive Agreements."

Sai. David Keanu. "Hawaiian National Sues President Obama in Federal Court in Washington, D.C." 5/31/2010.

Siu, Leon. "Commentary on the Hawaii Ceded Lands Case at the U.S. Supreme Court." Oct. 1, 2008.

Thurston, Lorrin Andrew. *A Handbook on the Annexation of Hawaii.* St. Joseph, Michigan, U.S.A., A.B. Morse Company, Printers and Binders. [1897].

Trask, Haunani-Kay. *From a Native Daughter: Colonialism & Sovereignty in Hawai'i.* Monroe, Maine: Common Courage Press. 1993.

Zalburg, Sanford. *A Spark Is Struck! JACK HALL & THE ILWU IN HAWAII.* Honolulu: University of Hawaii Press. 1979.

End Notes

Preface

1. "The Importance of Annexation to Kanaka Maoli Today" in *Self-Determination,* March 1998. Published by the Kanaka Maoli Tribunal Komike, sponsor of the 1993 Peoples' International Tribunal in Hawai'i. Honolulu.

Chapter 2 Brief Review of Hawaiian History

1. Sam Low, "Voyages of Awakening," in *Hana Hou*! Vol. 3, Number 1, February/March 2000.

2. *Dominion of the Hawaiian Kingdom*, a document prepared for the United Nations' Security Council as an attachment to the complaint filed by the Hawaiian Kingdom against the United States of America, 5 July 2001. David Keanu Sai I 1.5 (Author's note: This major source will be henceforth abbreviated DHK.)

3. Liliuokalani, *Hawaii's Story by Hawaii's Queen*, viii.

4. DHK, II. 2.1

5. Ibid.

6. Ibid.

7. Ibid. II. 1.r 2.51, 2.52

8. Ibid. II. i.r 2.53

9. Ibid. II. 2 2.66

10. Ibid. II.2 2.68

11. Ibid. II.2 2.72

12. Ibid. I. 1.19

13. Ibid. I. 1.25, 1.35

14. Ibid. I. 1.2, 1.30

15. Ibid. I. 1.31

Chapter 3 The 1893 Sneak Attack Overthrow

1.Liliuokalani, p. 210

2. DHK, III. 3.1-3.5

3. Ibid. III.1 3.7, 3.8

4. Ibid. III.2 3.10

5. Liliuokalani, pp. 387-388

6. DHK, III.2 3.14

7. Ibid. III.3 3.15, 3.16

8. Liliuokalani, pp. 235, 236

9. Ibid., pp. 376, 377

10. Ibid., pp. 386, 387

11. DHK, III.3 3.16

12. Ibid. III.3 3.17

13. Ibid. III.3 3.18

14. Liliuokalani, pp. 180-182.

15. DHK, III.3 3.20

16. President Grover Cleveland, Address to Congress, Dec. 18, 1893.

17. DHK, III.3 3.23

18. DHK, III.6 3.33

19. Ibid. III.6 3.35

20. DHK, III.8, 3.40

Chapter 4 Her Majesty, the Queen

1. Liliuokalani, p. 229

2. Ibid., pp. 233, 234

3. Ibid., pp. 278, 279

4. Ibid., p. 280

5. Ibid., pp. 281, 282

6. Ibid., pp. 323, 324

7. Ibid., p. 326

8. Ibid., p. 334

9. Ibid., p. 353

10. Ibid., p. 337

11. Ibid., p. 338

12. Ibid., p. 365

13. Ibid., p. 360

Chapter 5 The Annexationist Plot and Hawaiian Resistance

1. Lorrin Andrews Thurston, *A Handbook on the Annexation of Hawaii,* p.3

2. Ibid., p. 4

3. Ibid., pp. 4-6

4. Ibid., pp. 5-6

5. Ibid., p. 6

6. Ibid., pp. 15-16

7. Ibid., p. 21

8. Ibid.

9. Ibid., p. 27

10. Ibid.

11. Ibid., pp. 27-28

12. Ibid., p. 28

13. Ibid.

14. Ibid., pp. 32-34

15. Self Determination, p. 4

16. Ibid., p. 5

17. Liliuokalani, pp. 354-356

18. Ibid., pp. 369-370

19. DHK, IV.1 4.4

20. DHK, IV.1 4.5

21. DHK, IV .1 4.10

22. DHK, IV.1 4.11

23. Tom Coffman, *Nation Within: The History of the American Occupation of Hawai'i, pp. 69-70*

24. Ibid., p. 72

25. Ibid., p. 93

26. Ibid., p. 97

27. DHK, IV.3 4.18, 4.19

Chapter 6 Occupation

1. Noel J. Kent, *HAWAII: Islands Under the Influence,* p. 68

2. Ibid., pp. 70,71

3. Ibid., p. 72

4. Ibid., p. 77

5. Ibid., p. 76

6. Ibid., p. 85

7. Ibid., pp. 85, 86

8. Sanford Zalburg, *A Spark is Struck! JACK HALL & THE ILWU IN HAWAII,* pp. 144, 154, 288.

Chapter 7 The Allegation of "Statehood"

1. DHK, IV.4 4.24

2. DHK, IV.5 4.25

3. Ibid.

4. DHK, IV.5 4.26

5. DHK, IV.5 4.27

6. DHK, IV.6 4.30

7. DHK, V.5 5.32

8. DHK, IV.1 4.7

9. DHK, IV.1 4.8

10. DHK, IV.2 4.16

11. DHK, IV.11 4.44

12. DHK, IV.11 4.45

13. DHK, IV.11 4.48

Chapter 8 Hawaiian Renaissance

1. American Friends Service Committee (Hawai'i). FACT SHEET ON U.S. MILITARY IN HAWAI'I—JUNE 23, 2004

2. Ibid.

3. Ibid., citing *State of Hawai'i Data Book 2002*, Table 1.09—LAND AREA AND POPULATION DENSITY, BY COUNTIES AND ISLANDS: 2000.

4. Ibid., citing Defense Environmental Restoration Program Annual Report to Congress 2003. http://1163.88.245.60/DERPARC_FY03/do/home.

5. Ibid., citing Department of Defense Base Structure Report Fiscal year 2003 Baseline.

6. Ibid., citing *State of Hawai'i Data Book 2002*, Table 1.03 RESIDENT POPULATION, 1990 to 2002.

7. Ibid., citing Commander in Chief, Pacific Command, Briefing to Neighborhood Boards.

8. Joint Resolution of Congress, November 23, 1993

9. DHK, IV.7 4.31, 4.32

10. Marion Kelly, e-mailed report on hearing to author 6/26/04.

11. Ibid.

12. Ibid.

13. Ibid.

14. Ibid.

15. Keala Kelly, Opening Statement for Akaka Bill Forum, Aug. 23, 2005, held at Japanese Chamber of Commerce, Honolulu, Hawai'i.

16. DHK, V.12, 5.78, 5.79

17. www.hawaiiankingdom.org/vision.SHTML

18. DHK, V.12, 5.81

19. DHK, V.12, 5.91

20. DHK, V.12, 5.86 (See appendices A and B)

21. www.hawaiiankingdom.org., citing *American Journal of International Law*, Vol. 95 9 927

22. Ibid., citing *Chinese Journal of Law*, Issue 1 Vol. 2 p. 682.

Chapter 9 Parallel Paradigm: Liberating Lithuania

1. Dr. Albertas Gerutis, Editor. *Lithuania: 700 Years*, Translated by Algirdas Budreckis, pp. 143, 149.

2. Ibid., pp. 148, 149.

3. Ibid., pp. 155-158.

4. Ibid., p. 164.

5. Ibid., p. 196.

6. Ibid., p. 197.

7. Ibid., pp. 230, 231.

8. Ibid., p. 249.

9. Ibid., p. 337.

10. Ibid., p. 262.

11. Ibid., pp. 264-266.

12. Ibid., pp. 267-271.

13. Ibid., pp. 274-275.

14. Ibid.

15. Ibid., p. 278.

16. Ibid., pp. 305, 306.

17. Ibid., pp. 284, 285.

18. Ibid., p. 299.

19. Ibid., pp. 303-311.

20. Ibid., pp. 323-326.

21. Ibid., pp. 315-317.

22. Ibid., pp. 348-349.

23. Ibid., pp. 345-347.

24. Ibid., p. 347.

25. Ibid., p. 353

26. Ibid., pp. 353-355.

27. Ibid., p. 360.

28. Ibid., p. 370.

29. Ibid., pp. 373, 376

30. Ibid., p. 385.

31. Ibid., p. 386.

32. Ibid., p. 389.

33. Ibid., p. 398.

34. Ibid., p. 405.

35. Ibid., p. 407

36. Ibid., p. 413

37. Ibid., pp. 420-421.

38. Ibid., p. 427.

39. Ibid.

40. Ibid., p. 432

41. Richard J. Krikus, *Showdown: The Lithuanian Rebellion and the Breakup of the Soviet Empire*, pp. 94-95.

42. Ibid., pp. 47-48.

43. Ibid., p. 51.

44. Ibid., p. 53.

45. Ibid., p. 30, 54.

46. Ibid., p. 62.

47. Ibid., p. 63.

48. Ibid., pp. 63-64

49. Ibid., p. 64

50. Ibid., p. 71.

51. Ibid., p. 82.

52. Ibid., p. 83.

53. Ibid., p. 107.

54. Ibid., p. 108.

55. Ibid., pp. 109-113.

56. Ibid., p. 150.

57. Ibid., p. 153.

58. Ibid., pp. 153-155.

59. Ibid., p. 152.

60. Ibid., p. 98-101.

61. Ibid., p. 158.

62. Ibid., pp. 173-174.

CHAPTER 10 Contemporary Resistance in Hawai'i to the American Empire?

1. Koohan Paik and Jerry Mander, *The Superferry Chronicles: Hawaii's Uprising Against Militarism, Commercialism and the Desecration of the Earth*, pp. 41-42.

2. Ibid., p. 42

3. Ibid., p. 44

4. Ibid., p. 45

5. Ibid., p. 46

6. Ibid., p. 48

7. Ibid.

8. Ibid., p. 61

9. Ibid.

10. Ibid., p. 64

11. Ibid., p. 65

12. Ibid., pp. 87-88

13. Ibid., pp. 84-85

14. Leon Siu, “Commentary on the Hawaii Ceded Lands Case at the U.S. Supreme Court,” Oct. 1, 2008.

15. David Keanu Sai, Ph.D., 1893 Cleveland-Lili’uokalani Executive Agreements, p. 13.

16. Ibid., p. 4

17. Ibid., p. 5

18. Ibid., p. 6

19. Ibid., p. 36

20. Ibid., pp. 36-37

21. Press Release from Keanu Sai, Ph.D. “Hawaiian national sues President Obama in Federal Court in Washington, D.C.” pp. 1-2.

22. Ibid.

23. Ibid., p. 2

24. Ibid., p. 3

25. Ibid., p. 4

26. Ibid.

Chapter 11 As the Empire Crumbles

1. Thomas Naylor, “The Manifesto,” 1/1/05.

2. Ira Rohter, *A Green Hawai'i*, pp. 211-212.

3. Ibid., pp. 246-247.

Author

Jon D. Olsen is a self-described "unrepentant sixties radical activist" with "radical" not meaning violent or extremist, but the original meaning of "getting to the root of the matter." He grew up in Maine, getting a degree in philosophy from Bates College, and taught high school for one year. Discovering that while actual teaching was enjoyable, enforcing classroom discipline was not, he "escaped" to Hawai'i for the next 36 years. While there, and in the process of obtaining a Master's degree in philosophy, he was a founding member of Students for a Democratic Society, Resistance (to the Draft), and Peace and Freedom Party. A bit later he owned and ran a radical bookstore with volunteer labor of his own and others seeking a more just and peaceful society.

After a few short time jobs, including working in the Honolulu tuna cannery as a case stacker, a place where he met his newly arrived Filipina immigrant wife-to-be, he found a successful niche as a marketer of solar water heating systems, which he did for the better part of the next 20 years. He returned to Maine in August of 2001, as his father was about to turn 90 years old, and to reunite with the beloved family homestead adjacent to Damariscotta Lake where he had spent so many enjoyable hours fishing.

He quickly joined the Maine Green Independent Party and twice served on the State Steering Committee. Equally at home in Maine and Hawai'i, he has, from the mid 1970's onward, taken a keen interest in the latter's sovereignty movement, seeing it as an important part of the worldwide effort to defeat imperial rule, wherever it may be. He is the proud father of an adult daughter and adult son, and the grandfather of his daughter's two children.

CPSIA information can be obtained at www.ICGtesting.com
Printed in the USA
BVOW03s1243200214

345523BV00003B/8/P